THE LITTLE INFANT DESTINED FOR GREATNESS

DERIVED FROM THE ACRONYM THUG LIFE

KASHUS PETERSON

KCL GOODS

Copyright © 2021 by Kashus Peterson

All rights reserved.

No part of this book may be reproduced in any form or by any electronic or mechanical means, including information storage and retrieval systems, without written permission from the author, except for the use of brief quotations in a book review.

"4 I would rather be stricken blind than 2 live without expression of mind" - Untitled

Tupac Amaru Shakur

CONTENTS

Introduction	7
1. No Longer a College Dropout	11
2. Turning Lemons into Lemonade	15
3. Coming Out At 16	21
4. Hiding Behind "The Nation"	37
5. The Little Boy Trapped in A Man's Body	61
6. Didn't Ask to Be Here	69
7. Beginning Stages of Learning Thyself	75
8. We Matter	79
9. Jesse Williams Inspired Me to Be Greater	85
10. The Electoral College	89
11. The Beloved We Call Her America	93
12. Black Orator Impacting African American Lives	97
13. Mommy Too	103
Acknowledgments	109
Contact the Author	111
Bibliography	113

INTRODUCTION

The War on Iraq had not too long ago started, and I was 13 years old sitting at my end of the school year seventh-grade awards ceremony at Albany Middle School in 2003. They said the next award which was a writer's award for future authors or something to that effect would be physically be given later. Although they did not hand off the certificates at that moment to the recipients, we were still acknowledged for displaying exceptional writing abilities. I was not expecting anything I was practically a new student I had just started attending in January. It was damn near the end of the ceremony and mentally my mind was elsewhere, then I heard, "Kashus Peterson!". When I heard my name and walked on stage it had not clicked just yet in my mind. Honestly, I was just in school because it was a place my mother made me go to, I did not see myself as a writer, but I guess my language arts teacher noticed something about me that I had not yet discovered. I never actually received the certificate for the writer's award maybe because the next school year I ended up at a magnet school, to finish out my middle school career. For me, once I learned how to write a five-paragraph essay writing has always come easy, I am given a topic to write

Introduction

about and then I just go for it letting my mind run wild I have the ability to tell a story in great detail and I have been told my mind is like an elephant. I should have picked up on my gift of writing early, but it took for major things to happen in my life for me to realize my ability. I can attribute my gift of writing to my fourth-grade elementary school teacher at Adamsville Elementary School in Atlanta, Georgia back in the 1999-2000 academic school year. I do not remember her name, but my teacher was the one who gave me my first journal we used to write back and forth to each other every week. My teacher made it very intimate getting to know me by asking thought provoking questions that forced me to write more than just a few short sentences. To this day I wish I had access to my past writing pieces but due to trying to survive at the bottom all my most innocent and early writing pieces have been thrown away. It is okay that I no longer have access to my past works because my life has been a complete roller coaster and now, I am able to tell my story every chance I get there is no need for me to look at anything for reference my knowledge and memory serves me well making for remarkable stories to be told. This book is special to me because it is the first of quite a few that I will produce. Nowadays when I write it is for a purpose, it is a part of my therapy and meditation. I write to release hurt and pain. I write to complete required writing assignments for an A plus grade in my current college courses. As a child I was forced to keep my mouth shut so writing my feelings down on paper was my only outlet to express myself. I stopped journaling after my privacy was invaded twice and from there, I just held everything in. I never really had a best friend I could never stay in one place, so lifelong friendships are not something I am accustomed to. As a child I was quiet I did not have many friends at all and I felt like an outcast most of my years in grade school due to my home life, things just were not right. I was socially awkward and did not have anything in common with my peers. In this short book you

Introduction

will read about my life as a child and as an adolescent. You will also read thought provoking pieces that have been inspired from the knowledge I acquired from my upbringing. The purpose of this body of work is to motivate and inspire individuals to be great and always put their best foot forward no matter what. Brace yourself for these intimate pieces of my life that will surely go down in history as one of the best collections of essays from the last of a dying breed of mentally sane individuals striving to beat the odds and climb up the ladder to success. In my personal pieces names have been purposely left out, individuals who come forth to make themselves known will be doing so at their own risk I am not responsible for any damages or defamation of the characters you portray yourself to be in public, these are my stories, and I am sticking to them there is no need for me to tell lies my life is an open book for anybody that is willing to listen and read about it. Most millennials would rather get on a hot beat and speak about their life but that is not my calling in life I am too long winded. We are all artists in some way and my art is writing. I promise to tell the truth even if it cost my life because it is just certain facts of my life that I cannot make up and I no longer must keep quiet. This book is for the culture. This book is for that student that cannot seem to formulate an essay, take this as a manual to help you get an A on that paper by speaking from personal experiences or situations. Take this as a blueprint to help you create your big speech for class. It is a must I leave my imprint on this Earth because I know it is at least one person that will come across my book who will be thankful for the opportunity to have read my story because it will inspire them to tell theirs and possibly do better.

1
NO LONGER A COLLEGE DROPOUT

What put me on the course for my future? I got fired from my last job and decided to go back to school.

My life has been filled with much adversity I have had to overcome and getting fired from my last job made me realize I no longer wanted to be Kanye West (College Dropout) anymore.

Never settle the limit is not the sky.

My sexuality is not as important as getting a decent education to have a stable career in the future which is why I am back in school to finish what I started years ago in 2009.

Getting fired made me realize that I needed to get serious about the things that I am passionate about and it motivated me to enroll back in school to set me on the right course for my future.

I exercised my right to Freedom of Speech, and it caused me to lose my job which to me was a blessing in disguise because it prompted me to come back to school so that my livelihood will no longer be put into jeopardy due to me voicing the truth about racism and verbal abuse.

I felt as if it was my duty to be the voice for the voiceless thinking that once I brought what was happening to the forefront then something would have been done about it.

Stand for something or fall for anything.

After informing management that inappropriate remarks were being made to employees by their customers, I suggested that to make the employees feel secure and protected by their employer a newsletter or an automated message needed to be sent out to customers letting them know that our phone support agents were just there to help solve issues and verbal abuse would not and could not be tolerated.

My voice was ignored so I decided to take my voice elsewhere and that sent the message I had been trying to get out all along.

All in all they fired me but it made me stronger I was proud of myself and everything I stand for, it was a stepping stone for me because I was able to stand up and passionately say with tears in my eyes and a heavy heart "this is not right we are all human beings and at some point you have to draw the line and realize that we are all one race of people the human race it makes no sense to have hatred in your heart, in order for us to thrive in peace there must be love".

It is never too late to start over it is never too late to finish what you started take me as an example.

For the longest time after I decided to stop going to school, I never verbally admitted to anyone that I had no intention on coming back because I did not want to hear anyone's rant speech about how my little sister has a bachelor's degree and how I "let" her surpass me, it was all bullshit to me my only competition is myself.

It took for me to lose my job to realize that I needed to get back in school because for the last I guess six years plus I had been wasting my potential and intellect on things of no real importance, so I went back to the drawing board to secure a more stable future for myself and the family I gained in 2014.

This past fall was my first semester back since winter 2011.

If it was easy everybody would do it.

I came back to school and set the bar high for myself I said I was going to make all A's because I was never dumb I was just lazy and the thing with college is you have tons of unnecessary work and I had to decide if I wanted to make money full-time job hopping or take the time and do schoolwork, I was only 20/21 at the time when I made the executive decision to leave school to focus on work to pay the bills that would not stop coming.

Coming back to school full-time after a maybe six-year hiatus, I can honestly say in the beginning I felt a little nervous not knowing how I would pull it off, but I made A/B honor roll for the first time since high school because I never took my secondary education serious until now.

Getting fired was the best thing that could ever happen to me because it made me sit down and realize my true purpose in life.

It is not about money because when you do something you truly love the financial stability will come, education is important, and I am here to say it is not about where you come from it is about where you are going so, I would say work hard and do not let up on your dreams and goals in life **NEVER SETTLE** and **NEVER GET TOO COMFORTABLE.**

My major is history and Tupac once said, **"I may not change the world, but I will spark the mind that does"** and to me that is my goal in life it is to help people change their way of thinking by researching history and finding ways to make this life better than the previous I am Kashus Peterson and I am no longer a college dropout.

2

TURNING LEMONS INTO LEMONADE

By default, African Americans and/or the darker colored people have always been dealt the shit end of the stick when it comes to economics and wealth in America and around the world. Adversity should be the middle name of every black and/or dark complexion person that has had to overcome so many things such as, poverty, having only one parent or no parent for guidance, or making a way out of no way when all things seemed impossible to accomplish. "But ain't nobody gonna beat me at nuthin", a statement said by Sylvia in the short story "The Lesson by Toni Cade Bambara", speaks volumes to someone like me, whose life has been a complete roller coaster from the moment I was conceived.

"Ain't nobody gonna beat me at nuthin", there is so many simple meanings behind it. Despite all the bad in life there is still some good to be thankful for. When there is only darkness around have faith that there is light at the end of the tunnel. At times when circumstances are not the best do not complain about it, instead use that as motivation to better the circumstances. If the odds are against you, do whatever it takes to surpass the predictions because, "no one can beat you at nothing".

I was born to teenage parents, my father a drug dealer who has spent a great deal of my life in prison and other times just simply being a deadbeat choosing not to be present in my life. My mother an ambitious woman, a single parent (in my eyes), has relied on government assistance for as long as I can remember just to get by as far as shelter and food. Both my mother and my father no matter their decisions in life have always expressed to their children that they wanted us to do better and to want more out of our lives than their own.

I remember not having a bed to sleep on, yes, I slept on the floor palled it with blankets for a little bit of cushion and I remember not being able to go to school due to not having any warm clothes for the dry cold Georgia temperatures. Although I was not attending public school my mom stopped at nothing to make sure I was educated, even if it meant doing it herself. She taught me how to read and count money. Once my mom saved up enough funds, she took me to Goodwill and bought me warm clothes. She soon after registered me for school, I was in the second grade and during the holiday break she went to K-Mart and bought me one skirt and one shirt advising that it would be my uniform and I would be wearing it every day. My mom had rather lived poor than to let my dad provide for us with his illegal drug money and dramatic lifestyle. My mom took me from what I felt was a comfortable privileged life where I knew nothing about "the struggle" into a life of complete struggle due to her lack of finances. At that young age of seven I did not understand her reasons for fleeing from South Florida let alone "the lesson" she was trying to teach me. Education is important to my mom and as I have gotten older, I understand why she pushed me so hard academically and could care less about the material things because knowledge is everlasting and material things are temporary. Taking me from what I felt at the time was riches to rags taught me that "ain't nobody gonna beat me at nuthin", because if I am educated with a strong mind I can do and obtain anything the limit is beyond the sky.

My father sold crack/cocaine since the age of twelve, he was kicked out of school in the ninth grade for constant fist fights. He is the oldest of four children from his mother, and his father chose not to be actively present in his life. My grandmother tried her best to keep my dad out of the street life but after a certain point it was beyond her control. My dad was eighteen years old when I was born and out of my almost twenty-seven years of being on this Earth, he has spent at least eleven years incarcerated not including the three consecutive years my mother kept me away, all totaling out to fifteen years he has been absent from my life completely and might I add he is sitting in a Miami-Dade County jailhouse right now waiting for federal sentencing on drug trafficking and money laundering charges. My mother was sixteen years old when she birthed me, she dropped out of school and attended Hallandale Adult to obtain her high school diploma. She moved to Albany, Georgia in 1995 to start a new life and to get a college education. My mother did not initially take me with her at first, she came back to South Florida and basically kidnapped me from school in September 1997, she expressed in later years that she had to get out of the environment that she was surrounded by because she wanted better for her children. The fast money, in and out of jail lifestyle my father was living was not the life she wanted her children to be exposed to, even if meant having to be a poor single mother. She gave me guidance and life lessons to be able to get through life in an honest and righteous way. Both my parents are great examples of what I should and should not do as an adult and as a parent, their mistakes and failures have given me the blueprint of the life I want for myself and for my child. "Ain't nobody gonna beat me at nuthin" because I literally started from nothing and I am only dependent on myself.

When I was sixteen years old, I wrote my mother a four-page letter expressing to her that I was attracted to the same-sex. That was not the easiest news to share being that Islam is her religion and she had already expressed multiple times her dislike and disapproval against homosexuals. My reason for coming out was because I wanted her to let me move back to Florida. After a very serious physical altercation between her and I, my mother kicked me out of her house with just the clothes on my back stating that she wished had an abortion with me and that I was not allowed to take anything out of her house but myself. So, summer 2006 I moved back home to South Florida and started living in my truth, despite the bullshit my mother put me through all because she did not approve of my sexuality. Once I graduated high school, I had no other choice but to join the military for me to further my education because I had no legal guardian, my mother was not speaking to me and my father was serving a ten-year federal prison sentence. I enlisted in the Army Reserve for six years and I am now able to get a college education, so I can continue excelling in life. It has not been easy, a whole lot of blood, sweat, tears, and prayers have gotten me through because "ain't nobody gonna beat me at nuthin" only person I am trying to be better than is the person I was yesterday.

My life has been anything but a fairytale, but I would not dare complain because in my eyes I am blessed. I was not born with a silver spoon everything I have I worked hard for and earned it. "The Lesson" is a story that I can relate to because I was a child in poverty with limited resources and my mom could nowhere near afford to buy me a "$300 toy microscope". I someday will be a "Miss Moore", it is only right because my life will mean nothing if I do not use my success as motivation for younger individuals to want better and to rise above their circumstances despite the stereotype or label society has placed on them. When life give you lemons make lemonade, never give up because every day above ground is a blessing.

3

COMING OUT AT 16

I remember the first female I was attracted to her name was Stephanie we were in the same preschool class at Hallandale Adult Community Center where my mother attended school to earn her high school diploma/GED. As a child in school, I was very quiet I barely had any friends and I stayed to myself. I always allowed people to gravitate towards me because I was a socially awkward and shy individual. My life outside of school was full of confusion and disfunction leaving me to observe and absorb the things that were going on around me. Mentally forcing me to grow up quicker than I physically was and that basically is what left me to be an outcast not knowing how to interact with my peers because I was beyond my years. All throughout elementary and middle school I held a secret attraction towards females, but I kept it to myself unconsciously questioning myself on why my sexuality was abnormal trying to suppress my feelings because at the time I did not know it was an entire world of individuals who felt just like me. I would like to think of it as being aware with who I was at an early age. I remember most of my female crushes by name because it was not many, and it had to be something unique about her for me to like her and still to this day it is like that when I choose someone to pursue. I know most people have had some type of traumatic childhood experience that they blame for their attraction towards the same sex but that is not me. I have been very aware of my sexuality since I was child unable to articulate what I felt and at 16 desperate to be free and to live in my truth I wrote my mother a four-page letter coming out as a lesbian.

Up until officially informing my mom of my sexual preference I only confided into one person. My cousin knew my secret and accepted me for who I was at the age of 13. My cousin at the time being the only one I felt safe confiding in, encouraged me to tell my mom about my sexuality. I was 16 and highly annoyed with my life, I was on lockdown, my mom in her misery did not allow my sister and I to enjoy our childhood or teenage years we were under strict rules and supervision. One Saturday I found myself being a bit rebellious and instead of heading straight home after work at Sonic, I hung out with a friend who I felt was going to be someone who would show me the ropes in this same gender loving lifestyle more like a mentor. I honestly cannot remember her name, but she was cool and respectful. She was older than me like in her twenties had her own place, a car, a daughter, and would be considered a stud/dike like myself. That Saturday my friend picked me up from work and we hung out I drunk a wine cooler. I was not inebriated or anything the wine cooler tasted like straight juice I felt no type of buzz. Me feeling the need to brag and boast about having a drink and wanting people to know that I was getting down like everyone else on some lame shit, I lied to one of my homeboys and told him I was tipsy in a text message. My mom being the detective that she is, read through my messages and took my phone. She also made me quit working both of my jobs at Sonic and Chuck E. Cheese. She became way stricter than she already was, and it sent me into a rage feeling that I could no longer live my life being what I felt was a prisoner of hers.

While my mom was at work one day, I called my cousin venting my frustrations and that is when she told me "just tell her that you're gay so she can send you back to Florida". At that point I was ready and willing to let go of my secret because I no longer could take living under those circumstances, I had to force a change to take place that would give me some type of peace of mind. Prior to coming out my mom made the statement "if I find out any of my children gay, I'm going to disown your ass's", when my mom made that statement my cousin and I looked at each other with a smirk on our faces and talked about it later that night, like, "boy if she only knew the half". I was not expecting my letter to be four pages but four whole pages front and back telling my mother that her oldest child who is her daughter, is attracted to females and was ready to live life as an openly same gender lover. I was so scared to confront my mother I was too pussy to hand her the letter, I attached it on her car window as I walked outside to wait on the school bus one Friday morning. That Friday night my mother came home from work and had a whole attitude with me speaking very aggressive and eventually locking herself in her room for the remainder of the night. The next day on Saturday my mom went to work and came home that evening, she waited a little over twenty-four hours to address the letter with me and boy this woman made me feel like crap for taking the time to express my thoughts on paper. The woman (my mother) made me look up and read aloud the definitions of the term's heterosexual and homosexual. My mother made me feel as if she was trying to make a mockery out of me, at that point I was embarrassed feeling awkward as all hell standing up there reading having to start over because I was not reading "loudly and/or clearly enough", I was 16 years old I was very much aware of my feelings and there was no need for her obnoxiousness. After reading both definitions she asked me the rhetorical question "so are you gay?", I answered aloud and said "yes I like girls" as if she had not already read the handwritten letter numerous times at that point and as if that was not the whole point of us having this one-on-one meeting in her room. She sat in bed eating skittles as if she were at a theater watching a show, I felt naked standing at the edge of her bed feeling like my heart dropped to the bottom of my ass I was nervous and uncomfortable. She proceeded to ask a question in reference as to "why I felt like I liked girls" I tried explaining that it was just a feeling that I had, and I did not know why. At the time I honestly did not know how to answer that question not knowing that there was no right or wrong answer to that question I could have easily just said, "the same reason you feel the way you feel about who you're attracted to is the same reason for me as well it's just nature its natural for me". Answering the question like that she most likely would have jumped on me had I been able to think quick and be shady on my feet like that, but everything happens for a reason.

After not being able to I guess explain why I felt that I was "gay", my mother proceeded to come up with her own scenario stating that "you know what I think? I think when you lived in Florida with your daddy you and some little girl was doing things you had no business doing due to the lack of adult supervision". My entire life my mother has painted a picture as if my father and his family are bad news. With her false accusations I jumped to my father and his family's defense and said "no! That's not what happened at all and actually your mother (my grandmother) was the one who allowed me to do things to her when I was a little girl!".

It is true I did have an intimate encounter with my maternal grandmother, but I do not look at it as sex abuse and it is no way the reason, I choose to live the lifestyle that I do today. At about the age of about 3 or 4, I woke up one morning I found myself caressing my grandmothers' breast I am assuming I started doing it while I was sleeping. I may had been having a dream and somehow just woke up during it and got curious because I liked the softness of the breast rubbing on her nipples. At the time being that I was so young I was not aware that this grandmother was dealing with addiction, so most likely she was too high or drunk to properly discipline me. My grandmother changed positions in the bed multiple times getting up to leave the room coming back to lay on the alternant end from where I was but, I followed her to every spot she moved to because for that short time I was intrigued by what I was doing. She did not try to stop me or correct my behavior or maybe just maybe she was shocked at what I was doing. I feel like she kept changing positions in the bed so I could leave her alone, but I did not stop I do not even remember how it ended.

I grew up too embarrassed to tell anybody about that experience with my grandmother until I was forced to defend my father's family. I do not blame my grandmother for allowing that to take place no telling where she was in her life mentally and although I was a child, I knew I had no business touching her in that manner once I realized what I was doing. I do not blame my grandmother for me being attracted to females because I had already found myself being attracted to someone within my age range before I had even got a chance to explore a female's body. I was just attracted to beautiful women I was intrigued with pretty faces at a young age naturally.

For some reason with my mother reacting so quickly she did not give me a chance to fully go into detail, she did not ask questions she immediately acted as if I was a victim due to my tears, but I was never a victim. My mother in real life invoked fear and hatred in my heart for her so it was natural for me to feel anxiety, nervousness, and stress while in her presence so in a moment like discussing my sexuality please believe tears were falling and my words were stuttered which led to my mother's reaction. Without knowing the extent of what I had just said regarding my grandmother, my mom wasted no time as she assured me that everything was okay and that she was not mad at me, she called her mom and basically disassociated herself from her for violating her child. To this day to my knowledge my mother still does not have a relationship with her mother because of it and I strongly feel like she needs to let it go because for me it was not that deep. My grandmother has denied that anything took place, I do not know if she is lying or just do not remember. I know the truth and my story will never change. Remember I have the mind of an elephant a lot of things I will never forget.

Life after revealing that I was lesbian was empty for me at one point my mother said to me "I don't think you're gay I know damn well you're not gay you too pretty to be gay you just said that so I can stop worrying about you and boys I ain't crazy". It is like after she told her mom off my mother was not even thinking about sending me to Florida it was back to how things were, and I honestly was not happy with the outcome. I was ready to get the fuck up out of the lady house I was becoming restless being a homebody having to babysit and do chores all day every day.

After she found out about me drinking, she confiscated my other cell phone and was using them both as if they were hers. One night my homegirl (the older gay lady), called my phone and my mother cussed her out for no reason at all. I did not like the fact that my mother was rude to the woman, so I decided I was just going to run away and get back to Florida on my own. I had enough of my mother's shenanigans at that point. I just wanted to have a normal life with friends of my choice and to have freedom as I imagined it. The day after my mom cussed out my homegirl, I called a guy whom I considered to be my ex-boyfriend. I told him I was running away to his place that night so be on the lookout for me he said okay and that he would be up. I packed a bag and wrote my mom a note earlier that day on the back of a picture, I left it on my bed and dipped out in the middle of the night once everyone was asleep.

I know this is a "coming out story" but during this time in my life there was a guy who I conversed with, it was a school relationship we only talked and seen each other at school it could have been more, but my mom was too strict, and I was not going to take a beatdown from her for nobody so I stayed on my best behavior as best I could in her house. While at my ex-boyfriend house that night somehow, I almost lost my virginity to him. He had the condom on, but I would not let him go in, all I could think of was not wanting to get my hymen broken. As he was attempting to enter inside of me, I proceeded to help guide him in but as I looked down and felt him with my hand his penis size was too big for me and I immediately told him I was not ready I could not do it. He was not upset with me not wanting to have sex at that moment and I am thankful he did not just force himself on me. I think he understood why I was not ready, and he knew the things I was dealing with when it came to my sexuality. He did not care about my sexuality he was actually turned on by it, I think he honestly just wanted to freak me, and I was not with it we had our own issues to sort out amongst each other aside from this whole "gay" shit everybody was just finding out about. My stud/dike homegirl who my mom had cussed out lived down the street from my ex-boyfriend, so I ended up staying at her house the night I ran away.

The night I ran away from home I almost lost my virginity to a boy after coming out as lesbian, I smoked weed for the first time, but I did not get high, and I spent most of the night on the phone trying to convince this girl to let me come over her house until I was able to obtain the funds to catch a greyhound bus to Florida.

The next morning after running away the police showed up to my homegirl house and found me hiding in a dryer. I was handcuffed and placed in the backseat of a police car. I was arrested for running away and obstruction of justice. My mother had been trying to get me thrown in jail since the age of 12. The police did not want to hold me or file charges against me, but she forced them to place me on home confinement since there were no signs of me getting taken to the juvenile jail like she wanted them to. I was released back to my mom and placed on county supervision. Basically, at any given time throughout the 24-hour day, a social worker would show up at our house to make sure I was there. That day after getting released back to my mom, we got back to our house and she went off she gave me the words I had been praying for, "if you don't want to be here you can get the fuck out of my house". She spent all morning causing a scene making me out to be so unruly just so she could get me by myself to tell me that I could leave her house because she had other children to raise. The way I see it, shit I should have attempted to run away before my first attempt to run away. My mom took me running away for a few hours and dramatized it as if I were putting her through so much agony as if I was just a bad child. That was not the case at all I was tired of being her prisoner her slave basically.

After she told me that I could get the fuck out of her house, my mother called my great-aunt on the phone and exaggerated everything that was going on. She painted a picture so bad to the point when my great-aunt asked me was I gay I immediately retracted my statement and said, "no I'm not gay", my aunt response was "oh ok because I'm not with that shit". I said I was not gay because I was not ready for the uproar that came with it from people pretending to love me and acting like they wanted the best for me. My mom and my great-aunt made me feel like being myself was not okay and at that point I had to do what was best for my wellbeing in that moment. Had I kept saying I was gay my great-aunt would have never agreed for me to move back to Florida that summer in 2006. My grandfather picked me up and drove me to Carver Ranches, FL to be under the care of my great-aunt and I felt content, I was where I wanted to be.

As summer was ending, my mother after stating numerous times that I did not have to come back to Georgia proceeded to issue many verbal threats, stating that if I did not return to her Georgia home for the start of my junior year in high school, she would report me as a runaway. Had I been smarter back then a lot of the things my mother got away with would have been null and void. Being that my grandfather took time out of his schedule to drive to Georgia to pick me up, he advised my mother that if she wanted me back in Georgia, she would have to come pick me up on her own close to his home in Arcadia, FL before the end of July.

When I got in the car, my mother greeted me "As-Salaam-Alaikum", I did not feel like giving her the peaceful greeting back, so I just said, "hey mommy". She did not like the fact that I did not say "Wa-Alaikum-Salaam" and she clearly wanted to get to the bottom of it. Her husband made the trip to Florida with her and on the way back up he stopped in Lakeland, FL to visit his dad. We sat in the car while he visited with his dad and my mother took that opportunity to question me to the third-degree. The things that my mom was asking me I politely stated to her that I did not want to talk about, she told me "stay right there", got out of the car opened the van door and slapped me in my face about five or six times back-to-back with an open hand. I sat there and took the hits to the face because I was 16 and I knew that all of that would be over soon. I was furious and could do nothing but think about how I was going to get away for once and for all permanently. I had been coached to call the police each time her and husband placed their hands on me. I got back up to Georgia and got kicked right back out of the house.

My mother physically attacked me again and the police was called, she told the police that she no longer wanted me in her house and that I needed to find somewhere to go less than an hour after arriving back from Florida. The police officers who answered the call to come to my mother's house that night was rednecks, who clearly were racist against Black people. I had been physically attacked and they did not attempt to investigate or issue an arrest. They would not let me use any of their cell phones to make a call to get picked up. They showed no compassion or empathy about the situation, they truly showed that they did not care. My mother stated that the only way I could use her phone to make a phone call was if I gave her the metal and clear retainers out of my mouth. My mother knew that I was self-conscious about my teeth. One of my upper laterals never grew in leaving me with a gap in between two of my teeth, especially after my braces came off so she used that against me to break me down. I was so fed up I did not give two fucks about those retainers if it meant leaving her hell hole for once and for all I was delighted to give her those retainers packed with as much salvia as possible. I called my grandfather, and he was there to pick me up within twelve hours. While waiting on my grandfather to pick me up, that night my mother made me sleep on the floor and it felt like the AC temperature was turned all the way down, so I was freezing with no blankets. Early the next morning she woke me up and made me wait outside for my grandfather to arrive that afternoon.

I officially moved back to Florida in August of 2006, my great-aunt picked me up from my grandfather's home in Arcadia, FL. My great-aunt became saddened at the fact that my body was beat up. My hair had been pulled out from my scalp. I was walking around with a missing tooth. My physical appearance

The Little Infant Destined for Greatness

was the result of my mother showing that could not and have never been able to control her emotions.

After about a month I was awaken to who my great-aunt truly was. I eventually realized it was no better living with my great-aunt than my mother they both turned out to be my enemies. While under my great-aunts care I had to hide who I was, so with that came a boyfriend because it was something my great-aunt pushed on me. They had him already lined up for me, it is as if he was chosen for me. He was presented as a nice young man from the neighborhood who had his own car and a job with no girlfriend. I wanted to make my family happy but deep down I was not happy, because I was living a lie. A double life basically, I was in school being open with my sexuality and once I got home, I had this boyfriend I would spend time with, because in the words of my great-aunt "Kashus you're 16 years old you shouldn't be up under me you supposed to be with your boyfriend". It is as if my great-aunt wanted me to be a sexually active individual like herself who I later found out was like that at a very young age.

For my seventeenth birthday I got a cell phone, my great-aunt despised it and did not want me with it at all. I was responsible for paying my own phone bill, but I was not allowed to have a job. One morning at school before classes started for the day, an assistant principal confiscated my cell phone and the only way I would be able to retrieve it back was if the phone signed out by a parent/guardian. That day I was going to be staying after school because I was the manager on the girls' basketball team and needed money for food later. I called my great-aunt from the classroom phone in my homeroom and asked if could bring me money for food. She asked why I was calling from the school phone, I explained that I had got my phone taken away before the 0725 bell rang to report to class. My great-aunt came up to the school to drop off the money, she stated that "I don't care about the phone they can keep it". As my great-aunt handed me the money for my food, I walked her outside to her small pickup truck, I figured it would not hurt to keep asking her to get my phone back for me although she had already said no. I kept asking, I asked all the way until she got into her vehicle and placed it in drive slightly letting her foot off the brake pedal. I do not know what light bulb went off in her head to make her change her mind, but this lady placed her car back in park, and said "as a matter of fact I will get the phone", as she turned off the vehicle. She walked back into the school's office, signed my phone out and left without giving me my phone back.

Initially when my great-aunt took my phone, I was stressed the fuck out all throughout my first period class not knowing what to expect the next time I faced her, then I realized that I had a lock on my phone, and it was impossible for her to get into it without knowing my lock code or completely resetting the phone itself. I enjoyed my day at school, ordered me some hot chicken wings and made the executive decision to finally admit that "yes I'm a lesbian I like females". I got home that night and my great-aunt was ready with the twenty-one questions and all she ultimately wanted was the code to my phone. It got to a point where I told her, "you can keep the phone but I'm not going to give you the code". She asked, "what do you have to hide?". I said, "I do not have anything to hide I just don't want to hurt nobody". She proceeded to say, "you like what you like, I like what I like, you are who you are, and I am who I am". For me, I interrupted it as her basically insinuating that she already knew what was up me. I was highly annoyed and over the whole conversation between us. She had turned out to be someone, I found myself not being too fond of because of the immaturity and obnoxiousness she had displayed over the last five to six months of me being under her guardianship. She asked, "is it a girl?". I said, "yes" and proceeded to head to bed. She sat at the dining room table and she told me "I'm not going to tell the family you have to". I did not respond and for me that was not a statement to respond to because I never seen a heterosexual person announce that they were heterosexual. After not receiving a response from me she asked did a second cousin of mine know about my sexuality I responded with a no and very nonchalantly she said, "oh but I still want the code to this phone". I did not understand the point of her being so interested in my phone business, especially since she did not buy the phone for me and was not paying the phone bill. She was so adamant about wanting to be all in my shit, so I gave her the code to get her rocks off and went to bed because mind you it was late at night and I still had to be in school the next day.

At that point I wanted to spend as much time away from home as possible. One day after school while at basketball practice with the team, another great-aunt called me and flat asked me "Kashus are you a lesbian!?". I was so choked up and not in the position to talk about that I told her I would be home in a few and that I would talk to her then. She said something to the effect of "you can't live in the house with me I won't accept that". I responded by saying "okay I'll talk to you when I get to the house". I got to the house that evening and both my great-aunts were there the one that knew and the one that called me. My great-aunt asked, "so is there any truth to what I've been told?". I said "yes", I was done lying and I was done hiding. I wanted that burden to be lifted off my shoulders it was time to be free and be the person I have always been inside. Both my great-aunts stood and sat there in the kitchen just crying, one of them kept asking "why Kashus why?" They acted as if it was the end of the world.

What really offended me forcefully coming out to my father's aunts, is when my great-aunt asked me, "now will I have to be concerned with you being around my granddaughters?" Let me say this, **I can only and will only speak for myself**. Let me be

CRYSTAL CLEAR yes, I am a same gender loving female and I am very much attracted to females but **never get that confused with me being a pedophile.** I **ABSOLUTELY** despise people that prey on children. I feel as though **ALL CHILD SEXUAL ABUSERS ARE WORTHY OF DEATH.** A child's innocence is never to be taken away like that it is very ungodly, so I will never be involved with anything dealing with child molestation and/or sexual abuse that is something I do not believe in nor do I agree with. When my great-aunt basically equated me being homosexual to being a child molester having great concern about her granddaughter's wellbeing around me, I was heated and no longer wanted to be associated with that side of my family excluding the cousins I am actually cool with. My great-aunt in one instance said to me, "the best looking female and male out of all the great-grandchildren both like what they already are". She stated to me, "look at ******** we already know what he is going to be". I did not trust my great-aunts at all at that point, so I was forced to advise the remainder of my immediate family with whom I interacted with of my sexual orientation.

After getting downed and criticized about my sexuality I spent the weekend telling my dad's mother and his sisters and his brother the "news". To my surprise I was not met with criticism I was given wise words and guidance for this life. My dad's youngest sister from his mother told me "I don't condone that lifestyle but you're my niece and I love you regardless and with that life you have to have thick skin". My aunt made me feel at ease, I was not looking for acceptance, I wanted my mind and sexual preference to be respected, my aunt respected that.

After coming out to everyone like she wanted me to my great-aunt who I once considered and wished was my biological mother proceeded to mentally abuse me every day. She would say things like a man and a woman together is a beautiful thing anytime we seen some type of heterosexualism displayed somewhere whether in movies or in public out and about. She even advised me that one weekend she was going to take me shopping to get a whole new wardrobe full of skirts and dresses. I did not move out of my mother's house just to be faced with even more scrutiny I was done with the antics I just wanted to live my life as the free-spirited beautiful being that I am.

I told my great-aunt that I no longer wanted to live with her and that I wanted to live with my dad's younger sister. My great-aunt was upset but I did not know she would get nasty and take a page out of my mom's book. My great-aunt took all my clothes leaving me with nothing and even stole my social security card so she could claim me on her taxes that year. My mom and my great-aunt did me dirty they are two of a kind and I am just thankful to God for someone like my aunt to have taken me in. My aunt welcomed me into her home with open arms and allowed me to be myself while guiding me into adulthood. I moved with my aunt at the age of 17 with nothing but the clothes on my back in February of 2007 and to this day it was one of the best decisions I have ever made.

4

HIDING BEHIND "THE NATION"

When I was six years old my mother left Florida to attend Job Corps in Albany, GA. I remember the day she told me that she would be leaving for school but would only be taking my younger sister because I was over the acceptance age limit for childcare on campus. She left me in the care of my father's mother. I had no problem going to my grandmother's house because I was accustomed to visiting her frequently. I was left at my grandmother's house often because my parents were not in a relationship so the family they created together was never first. After a while, my mother eventually called to have my sister picked up from Georgia for whatever reason so we both ended up living with my grandmother for about a year and a half.

It was a September day in 1997 I will never forget hearing my name called over the classroom intercom at A.C. Perry Elementary School, for early dismissal and complete withdrawal. My heart dropped because the day my grandmother had warned me about months ago was here. I was frightened for my life because I did not want to go, I needed help, but I was not able to think quick. I was afraid to cause a scene I did not know what to do so I kept my composure and remained calm. While in route to the school office I was met outside the office doors by my mother's father, some guy who I later found out was her husband, and my mother who was visibly pregnant and was dressed in a way I had never seen dressed before. My mother smiled at me and opened her arms for a big hug. When I think of how I felt at that moment I just wanted to cry, I wanted to run away but I had nowhere to go I was trapped it was too late. I was in the second grade and had not lived with my mother since she had left me in the middle of my kindergarten year at Sheridan Hills Elementary School forcing me to transfer because my grandmother lived in Miramar, FL at the time. When my grandmother told me that my mother was going to be coming to pick my sister and I up to move to Georgia she did not know when it would happen, and I expressed that I did not want to go she told me to just let my mother know that and maybe my sister and I would be able to stay.

I was so use to my life the way that it was, and I cared less about living with my parents. My mother was a promiscuous woman who spent a lot of time doing her own thing leaving my sister and I to be kept by whomever was available and my father a drug dealer who I rarely seen but he always provided financially whenever he was not in jail which was rare. For me there was no emotional attachment to either of my parents for as far back as I can remember neither of them showed me much love, that feeling, "a mother's/father's love" I do not know what that feels like, that emotional connection/attachment. I was content with being with my grandmother because I was able to be a child, I always enjoyed life with her, and she showed me unconditional love.

That day when my mother withdrew my sister and I out of school, I found out that she was seven months pregnant and married. After they picked us up from school they went about the day as if what they had just did was normal. My mother acted like everything was all good, they went down to Miami to visit the mosque and some other family members on my mother's father side. At the time when we visited the mosque, Miami Nation of Islam mosque No. 29, I did not know what was going on or what happened to the mom I used to know before she went off to school not even two years prior. I was confused as fuck constantly hearing "As-Salaam-Alaykum and Wa-Alaikum-Salaam". Throughout that day I found out that my mother had converted to now being a Muslim and that her husband was also Muslim. My mother's husband did not say much to me and I did not have any words for me. I did not know him, but I did feel offended when a Muslim man at the mosque asked him, "is this your family Brother?". He responded by gripping onto my mother's stomach acknowledging that the child she was carrying was his. As far as I know my sister had already known him from when she was up in Georgia that short while and they had some type of bond. I know the question may have been awkward for him to answer but his answer displayed how rude and ignorant he is. My mother just stood there, and they all laughed it off awkwardly going onto the next subject. I wanted my grandmother I wanted to go home to my grandmother's house that is where my mind was that is where I felt whole.

After basically kidnapping my sister and I out of school for her own selfish reasons, my mother and her husband finally got us up to Albany, Georgia and life was not the same for me. I was sad I was angry I wanted to be back in South Florida. When we got up to Georgia it was cold, and my sister and I had no clothes. My father would not let my mother take any of our belongings he basically felt that since she had clearly moved on then that man should have provided for us, but as I soon realized that was not the case at all. My mother's husband was a broke boy coming out of Plant City, FL with a total of 7 children outside of the one he conceived with my mother.

The thing is while my mother was in school getting an education, my father was still financially supporting her. So, when she came down to Florida unannounced to take my sister and I out of school, she was pregnant, claiming to be married, and was now a Muslim. All of that was a shock to everybody no one knew what the hell was going on.

My mother and her husband had us living in a one-bedroom apartment at 920 W Society Ave Albany, GA 31701. It was infested with roaches and they made us sleep on the floor while they slept on just a mattress in the same room. My sister and I did not start school until she got enough money to take us to Goodwill for clothes. We were in Georgia for a few weeks before we started school in October then she gave birth to my oldest little brother in November of 1997 and that caused us to miss another few weeks because she left us in the care of one of the women in the mosque.

Life had changed drastically for me and my mother did not allow my sister and I to have communication with my father or his family. I vividly remember one day I was sad and for some reason I could not stop crying I was just hurt. I told my mom I wanted to move back to Florida I told her I did not want to be there, and she whooped my ass four times throughout the day. She really put her all into beating me, she would take me in the living room and just scold me while saying things like, "I'm gonna give you something to cry for", and "keep crying I'm gonna do this every time". I would describe that beating as child abuse in the first degree if that makes sense like first degree murder, I was seven years old and no one had never done anything like that to me ever especially not my dad or his mother. My mother frequently physically abused me and my sister. For whatever reasons her and husband called it discipline but today that is classified as child abuse if you use anything other than your hand to chastise a child. Had I been smart enough to call the cops back then I would have made sure my mother and her husband was not allowed near my sister and I ever again. The way that they beat us, was excessive and unnecessary most of the time. It is as if they wanted to beat our fondest memories of our father and his family out of us, they wanted us to detach from what we knew as home and force their ways upon us, like how Africans were brought over and made to be slaves forcing their identity to be stripped from them. We basically were in a unlearn to relearn processing method by any force necessary.

To add to the physical abuse, we had to endure along with the horrible living conditions, my sister and I was also subjected to having to frequently listen to our mother and her husband having sexual intercourse, they would tell my sister and I to get out of the room while they stayed behind and went to town on each other most of the day whenever her husband was not at work. One night I witnessed them in the act and when my mother noticed I was awake because I moved my head, she yelled at me telling me to go to sleep while her husband stepped out to go to the restroom. He came back in the room and she told him "I think Kashus saw what we were doing", He did not seem to care at all. One evening my mom was laying on his chest with a tee shirt and panties on and they began to get intimate in front of us, he placed his hand in her underwear and gently caressed her butt and would not stop. She told us to get out of the room and to close the door behind us.

I was so fed up with them and miserable one day I had packed up my small purple duffle bag of belongings that consisted of mainly toys and sat it by the door. I wanted to run away at that young age of 7/8 depending on if my December birthday had passed by that time. When my mother finally got through laying on her back or whatever she did to make her husband moan so loudly, she came out of the room looked around and noticed my bags at the door, she asked where I was going and of course I got beat that day.

Initially moving up to Georgia we walked EVERYWHERE we had no vehicle. I was not used to the life my mother forced on us at all. We ate navy bean soup to the very last drop in the pot. It was so burned up from being reheated I use to think roaches was in my soup. She forced us to eat it, we would have to sit on the floor all night until we finished the bowl. Sometimes I would try to swallow it to bypass the taste and end up gagging about to vomit just to hurry up and finish it. We were forced to eat leftovers while her husband brought home Arby's every night for them to eat. We did not have a choice, my sister and I had to eat whatever my mother prepared for us or we would be subjected to a beating on top of having to still eat the food.

My birthday is in the month of December and for my 8th birthday they did not celebrate it stating that as Muslims they didn't celebrate anything but the Day of Atonement in October and Saviours' Day in February. They baked me a pound cake for my birthday, but it was as if it was not even mines because my mom's husband ate most of it. Within that same month of December my stepdad sent a shit load of toys to his children for Christmas in Atlanta. My sister and I got excited when we saw the toys thinking they were for us, but my mother said no they were gifts for his other children. To this very day I still do not know or understand why my mother married this psychopathic deadbeat.

When my sister and I first moved with my mom and her husband they wasted no time trying to condition our minds to be Black Muslims. When asked to describe what was life like growing up with two people pretending to be righteous Nation of Islam members I would say they were and still are a part of a cult with the behavior they have displayed over the years, Nation of Islam owe me the last years of my childhood because I was forced and subjected to things I never saw coming. My mother and her husband have done nothing but struggle in all areas of their life since they introduced me to the teachings of Elijah Muhammad. We were poor as fuck I seen no blessings come out of my mother being a part of the Nation of Islam besides the fact that she uses the nation as her savior from her past lifestyle choices. Growing up in the nation as a child in school children use to make fun of us by calling my sister and I nuns seeing us in our headpieces because they did not know what Muslims were. It was embarrassing living in those conditions and not being able to tell what was going on because my mother frequently told us "what goes on in this house stays in this house anybody have a question tell them to ask your mother". My mother's husband made things no better for us as often he found humor in the things we had to endure. We were poor wearing the same thing to school every day to the point they implemented the mandatory wear of school uniforms the following school year going into the third grade.

Every year annually the Nation of Islam holds the Saviours' Day convention in February in honor of Fard Muhammad's birthday it is usually a three-day weekend event running from Friday thru Sunday. Saviours' Day was described as the "Muslims Christmas" by my mother but there was never a Christmassy feeling about it. Every year February we were mentally prepared to go up to Chicago, IL for Saviours' Day and every year except for one year we were let down, I did not go to Chicago until I was 16 years old, I had been waiting since the age of 8. The first Saviours' Day experience for me would have been in 1998. My mom went all out she had my sister and I first white Sunday garments made, she made bean pies, and had us thinking we were heading up to Chicago with the rest of the believers. My sister and I got home from school the day we were supposed to travel up to Chicago my mom told us that we were not going to go that year and that her husband had already left out on the road with the brothers.

My mother and her husband take being in the nation serious with all the years of obvious struggle they take pride in just being the help around the mosque acting like straight groupies whenever someone of "importance" is in town they are the first in line to put they life on the line to stand around and do security and conduct frisks of all persons entering into their place of worship. We were dirt poor but every Sunday they were giving up donations talking about it was to help the minister, I thought to myself plenty of times like "who's going to help us?". To keep my sister and I awake and alert in the mosque my mother made us take notes of the lectures. The person I was intrigued by the most was Malcolm X, and to this day I am still studying and learning about him. Whenever we were not in the mosque, they were teaching us to basically hate white people, they frequently trained us on how to defend ourselves when attacked.

Whenever we were not being force fed Islam down our throats my sister and I was subjected to staying in our room all day having to ask to use the restroom amongst other things we were told we basically could not move unless we asked or was told to do something. We were not able to play outside, and we had no relationship to the outside world. Going to school was our only form of entertainment and even still my mother had us believing that we were being monitored. Some days we did not eat at school breakfast or lunch because we were not allowed to eat meat. They told us we were vegetarians our diet was mostly bean soup, wheat bread, and water. It is crazy because in the nation they are taught to do for self but, my mother and her husband did the total opposite. I strongly believe that the only reason she wanted my sister and I to live with her is so that she could get government assistance, I am a food stamp section 8 baby I know the struggle. She had one of her Muslim "sisters" claiming my sister and I on their taxes every year. Every chance she gets, my mother bad mouths "the enemy" and uplifts "the nation" as if she has gotten anything out of the nation in the over twenty plus years, she has been in it. My mother spent all those years struggling praying for better days thinking Allah is going to magically drop something out of the sky to save her when she should have been putting all that energy into securing a future for her children.

My mother does not love my sister and me. She loves her children that her and her husband conceived more than she loves us. One night I observed the affection my mother gave my oldest little brother so sweet and gentle towards him while he slept and thought to myself like "wow that's the type of love I would like". My sister and I never got that affection from her instead we were beaten for everything even things we did not do. When I was sixteen my mother told both my sister and I "I should've got an abortion with both of ya'll ass's". My mom never showed me any type of love that I would consider "a mother's love", she used my sister and I as meal tickets to take care of her husband and their little family. Our presence was just for convenience to get more assistance and to work us like slaves, we cleaned up behind everybody and had to babysit frequently. My mom would go grocery shopping and all the snacks would be theirs. My sister and I were not even allowed to eat any of the snacks, one day my mother found a chip in the toaster and since neither my sister or I confessed to dropping a potato chip in the toaster, my stepfather went and pulled a switch off the tree and made my mother beat me and my sister for something to this day we both deny doing. Lying was forbidden and we did not lie but they did not believe us so we got scolded for no reason it was one of the worse ass beatings ever I will never forget the stings of that switch hitting my ass laying across their bed, my sister and I did not deserve that.

My mother's husband would be described as a psychopath and when I asked her why she chose him over my biological father she basically said that my biological father could not make her have an orgasm like her crazy ass husband and that her husband made her feel like a woman. At the age of 16 she got pregnant with me she had no business having sex so that was a poor excuse. Both my father and her husband are physically abusive she should not have been with either of them.

When my mother finally got approved for her section 8 voucher, we moved into a public housing townhome complex, the first night we got there she told my sister and I, "since we're in a new place now ya'll can't call him by his name, ya'll have to put brother in front of his name or call him daddy". I was almost 9 years old and very aware of who my biological father is. "Daddy" is the name I called my father so there was no way for me to call this man who barely interacts with me and my sister and has made my mother cry numerous times at this point "daddy". Hell no I was never going to call him "daddy", because he is not my daddy and when he had the opportunity to claim my sister and I he did not so no. I was so afraid of the beatings back then because my mother was unable to control her emotions when it came to us she used all of her physical strength when chastising us. Not knowing what her reaction would have been if we declined to call him daddy my sister and I said we would call him daddy and my mother told us to go and ask him was it okay, we asked, and he said yes. It felt so staged like he told my mother to do that, if he wanted to be addressed a certain way, he should have been introduced to me that way. From the moment my mother pulled that stunt with trying to make her daughters call another man "daddy" I had no words for her husband, it went from awkward to awkward and weird as fuck living with those two crazies. I never not once uttered the word "daddy" when speaking to my stepfather I just use to start talking if I had something to say to him but that was very rare. I wanted nothing to do with him and he never tried to build a relationship with us so that we would feel comfortable enough to look at him like a father figure he was just there. He was so rude and sexist he had no respect for women not even my mother who bore his two sons. My sister and I were living in boot camp while in the guardianship of our mother and she frequently would take whatever anger she had out on us yelling at us and beating us for unnecessary things, making us do squats and other exercises as discipline. My sister and I were not bad children at all if anything we were too good. I often would cry myself to sleep not wanting to wake up another day and each day just got even more depressing. Our childhood was ruined our life was dysfunctional and I often wondered if my family in Florida thought about and missed my sister and I like we missed them. We needed to be saved and we did not know enough to escape no one was on our side my mother and her husband had everybody fooled about our life, we were in prison.

One night I was awakened out of my sleep due to my mother's husband yelling and punching holes in the walls. I woke my sister up and told her they were in their room fighting and shortly after the police arrived, I guess the neighbor heard my mother's cries and the loud noises and could not sleep. When the police got inside the house, they wanted to see my mother who was carrying her second son from her husband at the time. My mother denied that she had been assaulted and her husband's only concern was that my mother needed to get dressed before he allowed the police to enter their room to see her. Being that she denied that her husband hit her, the police could do nothing. They did not ask questions to see if anyone else was present in home at the time no one even stepped foot in our room. Had a thorough check been conducted, I surely would have told the police what I had witnessed just from laying there in the room listening to the exchanges. The next day after the fight and as time passed on there were visible holes in the walls throughout the house where we lived from my deranged stepfather.

At an early age my mother exposed all her children to her unhealthy relationships and marriage. It is as if my mother placed blame on herself for her husband's reckless behavior. Behind closed doors her husband is a devil a monster and needs to be in a cage where he belongs. He has physically assaulted both my sister and I on some serious psycho shit I promise he has never put hands on his biological daughters the way he put hands on me and sister he deserves to be put away for what he did to us. He went on countless rants very often along with his physical abuse he treated my mother like shit, and she let him she would not even defend us her own daughters but wants us to bow down and worship the ground she walks on all because she reluctantly gave birth to us. One day coming home from school my mother was visibly saddened, he told us to get ready to go as he asked her "you want to go back down there with your daddy?", my mother did not respond, and we all left. We got to this place, I am assuming it was somewhere for them to get a divorce, but it was not the courthouse, he walked around the office and told us to lets go, it was a scare tactic. If those two were not having sex like rabbits he was beating her up and calling her out her name constantly reminding her that "you don't know me". After that moment where I guess he was giving her the ultimatum to stay or go, shortly after we moved to Atlanta, GA.

Moving to Atlanta was like a dream of theirs. The south regional headquarters for the Nation of Islam, mainly his dream because my mother only wanted to do what he wanted to do she wanted to be one with him always which is why she was so disconnected from her daughters. She did not care about how we felt about anything she never even asked. It went, her husband, her boys, the nation, then her daughters that was my mother's life she did not give a fuck about my sister and I she literally treated us like property. Moving to Atlanta did not make life any better for us, the Atlanta mosque was bigger and had more people, if anything moving to Atlanta made me realize how poor we were compared to other Muslims. Every family seemed to have their life together besides ours. One day my mother broke down and cried because she did not have us prepared for a Mother's Day event amongst the sisters one Saturday. All the mothers and their daughters had matching tea sets and stuff and my mother gathered us up to leave. One sister stopped her in the hallway and spoke with her letting her know that it was okay and that it was extra sets available so either way we would not have be left out. Had my mother been attending her weekly MGT meetings every Saturday like she should have she would have known what we needed, but her and her husband was in Atlanta struggling. He kept deadened jobs and my mother acted as a "housewife" for the longest time. One good thing about the Mother's Day event and I am glad we did not leave is because I was able to recite a poem I had been practicing for that event and day, the applause I got from it was very heartwarming.

In Atlanta, my mother and her husband would lock themselves in the room all day on a Saturday and have sex we would hear them moaning and groaning very often to a point where it traumatized me. I felt disgusted with my mom and her husband they held no regards for us. To keep us occupied while they had sex my mother would make my sister and I babysit my younger brothers and read books and write essays all day long whenever we were not at school.

Over the course of almost three years, I can count on one hand how many times my sister and I spoke to our biological father it was not often at all and when we did speak to him my mother would sit on another phone and monitor the conversations. She would make us write letters to our dad, but I knew he would never write back my father is not that type of man. One day after school on my sister's birthday May 25,2000 we got home, and my mother told us we would be going to spend the summer with our dad in Florida. I cried tears of joy I had not seen my daddy in so long and out of nowhere we were just leaving with no warning. She had us pack dirty laundry to take with us stating that they would have to wash our clothes when we got down to Florida. I do not know what my mother reason was for sending us off but all I knew was that in the back of my mind I was not going back no matter how much I liked the Atlanta atmosphere I hated living in the house with my mother and her husband. I knew life was better in Florida and that is the life I wanted for myself. I was not born to be a babysitter and to be a live-in maid for my mother and her husband I wanted out. My mother did not allow my father to pick us up from where we lived instead, she had him meet us at a hospital around the corner from our house as if where we lived was a big secret. Both my mother and father had clearly moved on both having two outside children each that are all the same age two born in 1997 and two born in 1999.

My sister and I got back to Florida and life was not so bad. When my mother started calling for us to come back home, I expressed that I did not want to go back, and my father told me that I did not have to. My sister was put on a plane back to Atlanta and to this day I regret letting my sister go back to Georgia by herself. My sister is about two years younger than me and at the time I was 10 years old and she was 8 I was not supposed to let us get separated like that. I was a selfish individual only thinking of ways for me to have a better life when I should have had my sisters back, we were supposed to stick together, and I dropped the ball I still haven't forgave myself. I could have been a better big sister, but I could never focus on the present it was always me living in the past and thinking about the future.

The day after Thanksgiving in 2002 my mother showed up at my father's house with the police to come get me in the middle of the night. I was awakened up out of my sleep, "Kashus your mama outside with the police". My mother strategically showed up to our house late that night thinking my father would not be home because it was no secret that he sold drugs and his working hours was the graveyard shift. I stepped outside to see what was going on, my mother was basically telling the police that she wanted me to go with her and that if I did not go with her, she wanted them to take me into custody for being a runaway. The police explained to my mother that without a child pickup order there was nothing they could do since my father was present in the home at the time of arrival. My father explained to my mother that trying to put me in jail would not do anything to me because they both had been in jail, he told her that she would just be turning me onto to a life that I could mentally handle because they both handled it well. My mother left that night without me. I knew she was not leaving Florida without me the war was on. For a few days I stayed in hiding and someone tipped my mother off to one of my locations and I had to escape out of a window when she came back knocking with the police. I was literally running for my life trying to escape that woman asking total strangers could I hide inside their place. One lady said, "your mama coming to get you?", I did not even know the lady I knew her face from around the way but had no interaction with her. It's like everyone knew what was going on, people talk entirely way too much they do not know how to mind their business hence the reason why my mother knew every location to find me. The lady ended up letting me go into her house until it was safe for me to leave. My mother eventually was able to get ahold of me and served my dad court papers for a custody hearing. She was granted a temporary custody order for me until the court hearing. My 13th birthday was the worse, my mother could not leave the state until the hearing, so I was still in Florida. While awaiting the custody hearing, my mother kept me out of school. My mother was literally acting as if I were on some rebellious shit painting me out to be some type of threat to the environment, she would not let me out of her sight. For about a week or longer we were back and forth between my mother's father house in Carol City, FL and with my mother's family members down south in Perrine, FL until the custody hearing.

I hoped and wished the judge had granted me to stay with my father and my wish almost came true but once my mother realized that the outcome would not be in her favor she blurted out, "well I don't think he's her father anyway!". My heart dropped I became angry, the judge stated that until paternity was proven by default I had to go with my mother. That day in the hearing my mother proved that she would stop at nothing to have me in her possession and to this day I say that she only wanted my sister and I to get government assistance and to be able to sell our social security numbers at tax time. Living with my mom I seen it as a punishment. She even lied to me to make me feel better about moving back up to Georgia with her telling me that my best friend from the third grade stayed next door to them, because from the time I had left Atlanta they had moved back to Albany, GA. After the judge gave my mother sole custody of me, she wasted no time getting out of Florida we were on a greyhound bus back to Georgia less than eight hours after the custody hearing. While on the bus ride she came and sat next to me. I only wanted to know, "why did you tell them that he isn't my daddy?", she stated, "because I want you with me, you're my daughter and you need to be with me, your daddy wasn't raising you he was letting his girlfriend raise you". My mom did not know a damn thing about what was going on in my life with me living with my father, all I know is people have always been envious of me for whatever reason so no telling what lies she had been told. I was the golden child honestly multiple family members wanted me with them and since they could not have me, they wanted me to suffer with my mother. The envy and jealousy, it was real amongst my family when it came to me. On the bus that night my mother explained to me that there was another guy who thought he was my father, but she assured to me that my father was who I had always known him to be. My mother took it that low all so she could get her other maid and babysitter back under her roof.

When we got back up to Georgia it was just us. My mother, my sister, and my two brothers. My mother advised that her husband was in Atlanta and from what she had told me they were separated. That separation did not last too long because not long after I got back up to Georgia he was back in the house. Things had drastically changed when I moved back with them. They were no longer vegetarians now eating chicken and turkey.

My mother kept her hands off me for the most part once I moved back at the end of 2002. Since she knew I did not want to live with her, she decided to get my sister and I evaluated for mental disabilities as if something was wrong with us for not wanting to be with her. She had us going to counselors and seeing psychiatrist, the experience was humiliating for me because I was clearly in my right mind. She was going through desperate measures to control my mind and way of thinking. When a counselor asked my mother, "are there any family members from either side that suffers from mental retardation?", my mother quickly said, "yes on their father's side". Yes, my father did have an uncle (my great-uncle) who passed away that was mentally disabled, but my mother completely left out the part that she in fact have multiple family members who are mentally ill. At the time I did not know about the multiple members of my mother's mom side of the family suffering from mental illness because my mother is very good at hiding things, she does not want people to know about. I found out about my mother's family when she invited me to escort her to her grandmother's funeral in 2012 when I was 22 years old. I observed at **LEAST** three individuals that clearly showed signs of being mentally retarded one includes my mother's own brother whom I had never met before. Turns out when she had my IQ tested, I scored a little above average meaning I have a high level of intelligence. I was so angry and resentful towards my mother for putting me through that. My mother knew absolutely nothing was wrong with my sister and I mentally to that extent of suffering from mental retardation. She was being very malicious and vindictive like always and was just trying to benefit financially from the government if something was in fact found to be abnormal. I know how the game go she just wanted a check and was willing to sacrifice her daughters to get it. I say sacrifice because my mother is a part of the biggest black organization that is supposedly a threat to the United States government, but there she was running to "the white man" ready to shove all types of medications down our throats just so she could collect a check and mind fuck my sister and I even more. I wonder what her superiors in the organization think of shit like that. My sister at the time was the only one mainly subjected to my mother's physical abuse. My mother frequently put hands on my sister a lot of times for no reason doing things based off my little brother's tattle-telling lying and shit.

My mother's husband at this point (2003-2006), was in and out of the house every six months due to their constant fighting. Being that I was older now moving back with them I was not going to allow her husband to just beat on her in front of us or anywhere I was present I was ready to speak up and revolt against him. One day he tried manhandling my mother. They were arguing, and she attempted to go outside he yanked her back in by her shirt causing her to grab onto the wall for support to keep from falling. In uniformity I rose along with my sister and my cousin and I shouted at him to leave her alone as the three of us walked towards him ready to jump his ass if we had to. My stepfather was shocked he was so mad, he yelled at us making a sexist statement, "ya'll better not ever stand up to no man ya'll can't do shit to me". We could not do shit to him but he damn sure was not about to do shit to us either not that day I was not having it. From then on, he never tried putting his hands on my mother in front of me again. One Saturday when I was 14 years old, I will never forget I was in the eighth grade my sister in the sixth grade like always we were bored in the house because we never went anywhere, naturally, I am a goofy person who sometimes can get a little annoying I was playing around with my sister and she yelled out "stop Kashus!", we would yell at each other sometimes to try to get one another in trouble. When my sister yelled at me to stop, my mother called us both in the living room and made us do squats. I was not with that shit I did not feel like it was that serious for us to be squatting. My mom and I had an exchange of words back and forth, she was telling me to bend my legs more and I was basically telling her I did not want to and was trying to explain to her that my sister and I was just playing around I was not being disrespectful at all. My stepfather felt the need to chime in the conversation stating that me talking to my mother "was not cute", I told him "I'm not trying to be cute me and my sister was just playing, and it is no need for us to be doing knee bends". By me talking back to him he felt he had to prove something he had built up aggression and anger towards me, he yelled at me and I uttered those words "you're not my daddy!". It is as if he was waiting on that moment for me to say that to him, he wanted a reason to put hands on me. He got up and basically dragged me into the room while saying, "I am your daddy and I'm going to beat your ass I am your daddy!". Him and my mother beat my ass until my body was black, purple, and blue no exaggeration. It felt like the beating lasted forever in that room trying to fight them off me I was not even 100 pounds. I eventually gave up because the more I showed no signs of backing down the beating got worse, they took turns hitting me at one point holding me down while the other literally beat me. My sister told me to go to school on Monday and report it. As I sat in the bedroom that my sister, an older cousin and I shared I cried to myself that night because I was so badly bruised and it hurt my heart seeing my thighs beat up and barely being able to sit on my butt, my body was sore. My mom walked in and asked me why I was crying as if her and her husband had not just spent about thirty minutes earlier that afternoon taking turns beating up on me with belts, a metal hanger, and closed fists. I asked her why she allowed that man to put his hands on me stating that I do not even know him. With a puzzled look she asked, "you do not know him?", I responded "no I do not know him he even tells you that you don't know him", I was speaking of the numerous times I overheard them arguing. She just sat there and looked at me as I pulled off my clothes to show her how badly I was bruised especially all over my thighs they were literally purple and black. The next day on Sunday she took me to Walmart to get my glasses fixed because they had been broken from me wrestling with her husband the day prior and she got me some hot wings from the deli as a peace offering. I do not know why I did not report it to the school, but I should have that would have been my sister and I ticket out of there. Before I made drastic moves like reporting my mother and her husband for the unlawful treatment of us, I mainly use to think of my brothers like "who would raise them if they were to get taken away?". I knew it would have been nothing for my sister and I to go back to Florida with our relatives. Crazy thing is I had an orthodontist appointment that Monday after getting beat that weekend, so my mother made sure she came to pick me up from school and questioned me about if I had said anything to anyone. The more I think about shit the more certain people should be thankful to God I have always been in my right mind and that I think about the consequences before doing things. Had I not been such a sweetheart I honestly believe together my sister and I would have seriously hurt my mother and her husband. We let them get away with too much and only God knows the type of anger I hold in my heart for my mother and her husband.

They hid behind the Nation of Islam under the leadership of Minister Louis Farrakhan we were abused physically, mentally, verbally, emotionally, and spiritually. Every chance my mother gets she uses the man who they consider to be Allah aka Master Fard Muhammad as her scapegoat. Every chance my mother's husband gets he quotes Elijah Muhammad as his scapegoat. They are real live hypocrites. I call my mother a hypocrite because she was extra strict on my sister and I we could barely have friends, so boyfriends were out of the question and we were locked away in the house most of the time. As members of the Nation of Islam, Muslims were forbidden to celebrate pagan holidays. My mother has two sons both were born in the nation even legally holding Muslim names, my mother allowed my brothers to have girlfriends at a young age and even allowed them to participate in pagan holidays. She went out to buy Valentine's Day gifts to give to the little girls they showed interest in but when my sister and I were coming up we went from one world to another without any explanation and was damn near beat to death when we showed any sign of weakness as the holidays crept around. I remember waking up every Christmas morning yearly just to look out the window to watch as other children played with their new toys and rode on their new bikes. It was the worse going back to school after holiday break, everybody was rocking new clothes and shoes except for us. My sister and I were the less fortunate ones having to answer questions we could not really explain because our peers knew nothing about being a Muslim. My mother only threw that Muslim shit out there when it was convenient for her, she used Islam to cheat us out of having a fun normal childhood and teenage years. Being in the Nation of Islam is used as a coverup for a lot of things when it comes to my mother over the years, I have come to realize that everything she has always tried to portray me out to be, it is really her and that is also why she use to chastise my sister so much because my sister was too much like her but worse. I say my mother's husband is a hypocrite because he hides behind the teachings of Elijah Muhammad for protection because of his fucked-up ways, he will forever be a psychopath to me. All he did was cheat and beat on my mother, he brainwashed my mother he made her into his puppet for his own beneficiary reasons. He is not a real man he barely kept a job and is way too controlling. He disrespected my mother often also allowing my brothers to be the same way towards her. My mother's husband is the reason why my mother kept my sister and I away from the only people that loved us our family in Florida.

I know that no one is perfect but understand this, being a Muslim, you are basically taught that you are the best and must always act as such. My mother and stepfather together are not the Muslims they took the oath to be they backslide more than Christians, they are not the Muslims they portray to be in the presence of non-Muslims. They both use Islam to make excuses for their ill ways and ignorance enough is enough, the Nation of Islam is supposed to be a group of people that uplifts and motivates each other to be do and be better. All these years have passed, and I see people in the Nation of Islam treating it like it is no longer a sacred organization. I remember when being a Muslim was not cool now all of a sudden it is as if anything goes a bunch of clout chasers and when it is convenient, they just hide behind the Nation. My mother and her husband did everything they could to break my sister and I, but it did not do anything but make us stronger and motivate us to suppress the limitations they tried place on us. I do not hate the Nation of Islam and the teachings of the Honorable Elijah Muhammad, but I do hate that the Nation of Islam allows its members to hide behind that star and crescent flag pretending to be righteous people but monsters behind closed doors. Stop hiding behind "The Nation".

8/8/2020 – "Hide Behind "The Nation"" was written at the end of the year 2017 after an August fallout between my mother and me. During that time of my life in 2017 I was in a midst of my own internal battle, I needed healing. After writing this piece I realized how hurt, sad, and neglected I felt, it was definitely an eye opener. It was time for me to do the internal work and make self-changes to live a peaceful and more prosperous life. I have been able to heal and get over the stressful childhood that I experienced because in the year 1997 my mother was 25 years old and her husband was within the same age range. I had to let that shit go and be better I cannot change what happened in the past I can only create a better future for myself. Life is everything that you make it to be, karma is real so put out good karma to reap those benefits. At this time, my mother and I are in a way better place, I ask God and the universe to please continue to guide our journey as we grow and love each other unconditionally as mother and daughter should. **We Are Healing Now.**

5
THE LITTLE BOY TRAPPED IN A MAN'S BODY

When I told my father that I was attracted to females he asked, "who's Junior to you!?", not knowing the point of that question I answered, "your son my brother" sarcastically. After answering his question, with sternness in his voice he said, "exactly that's your brother you're not his brother!". What he stated was true, but the thing is, my father was in federal prison serving a ten-year bid for cocaine distribution and had not seen me in over five years. I was confused on how he just knew the route I was going shit I could have been a lipstick lesbian for all he knew.

To this day I feel like coming out to my father was a dream of his that he never wanted to come true. His reaction to me is confirmation that he had to have seen it in me as a child possibly, it went to show that it is not only boys with a little too much flamboyancy that you can sense will grow up to be homosexual sometimes but if you pay close attention you can sense it in your daughters too as a parent. I did not know what to expect telling my father that his oldest child was attracted to the same sex, but I must admit he was not as obnoxious as my mother. He basically told me that if dating boys was not my thing at that moment, I was not obligated to engage in that behavior, but he did not want me to be homosexual basically he was not condoning it.

I feel like in the black community next to being killed by a white racist, a parent's biggest fear is their child choosing to be homosexual. It is embarrassing to them mainly because nine times out of ten they have spent most of their lives frowning upon homosexuals whether directly or indirectly, so when their child comes out as homosexual it is like a slap in the face to them and they go to praying and asking God for forgiveness and automatically feel like they are being punished. Apart of the reason I feel that my father knew that me growing up to be lesbian was a big possibility is because I always admired him, I admitted to wanting to be like him. I was a tomboy he always bought me sneakers and my most favorite outfit he got me was a Chicago Bulls Michael Jordan jersey set with the patent leather black and red 11 Jordan's to match for Easter back in 1997 before my mother kidnapped my sister and I out of school. I always knew what I would grow up to be, but I guess my dad knew too and just ignored hoping that I would grow out of it but nope my mind had been made up for a long time. In between spoiling me and giving me most of things I asked for while in his care, my father has spent a great deal of my life incarcerated.

Word is my father started running the streets as a child and started selling drugs around the age of 12. He has spent a great deal of time in and out of jail from his teenage years up until now, he is damn near 50. My father was born to a teenage mother and his father denied him for a long time until paternity was proven. My father's father basically started coming around when he seen an opportunity to get rich. As a young boy my dad had an accident where his leg was cut open at a city park, so a lawsuit was filed. My father is a fatherless child his dad did not make much of an effort to be in his life let alone put in the time to show him how to be a man and make a legitimate means of income to take care of his family. I will not play the blame game but what I do know is boys need real men in their lives that will encourage them to succeed and groom them into becoming real good men. It is heartbreaking and embarrassing to know that my grandfather had the means and the legitimate resources to help his son grow into the man he once had the potential to be. It is easy to give the lame excuses like "oh his mother wouldn't let me around him all she wanted was the money" or "he never wanted to listen to me he was hardheaded". Those excuses are straight manure if you really want to do something in life you do it no matter how many obstacles you face. Every real man should want to be in their children's lives, especially their sons. I feel like my father was fed the short end of the stick and it caused him to miss out on being a real father to his children.

My father not having his father in his life led him to turn to the streets to raise him because after a while my grandmother was just tired of trying. She needed help in guiding her son. My father not having a legit father figure in his life hindered him from becoming a real man. My father is what some would label as a street nigga, he is all about making money and has a demeanor of one that is not playing games far from friendly so not a conversationalist and will use violence if need be to get his point across when tested. I remember the first time I seen my dad cry I could not believe it I did not know males cried until I seen my father cry. It was not the fact that he was crying it was the reason why he cried and how he went about shedding those tears. My grandmother told my father that she could no longer care for her mentally ill brother and had to put him in a home, that is why my dad was crying. When my grandmother told him about our uncle he went in the house and me being the inquisitive child that I was after a few minutes perhaps I walked in to see what he was doing because enough time had passed so I knew he was not taking a piss. As I stepped into the hallway, I seen him standing in the bathroom mirror crying it was not just tears coming out of his eyes he was literally crying. I ran outside and told my grandmother that my dad was in the bathroom crying. My grandmother went inside and told my father that she could no longer handle talking care of her brother and that no one was helping her, so she did not have a choice but to put him in a place to be supervised. Up until that point I had never seen my dad show emotions like that the most I had seen him do was beat my mother's ass a few times. I was too young to understand the reason behind him putting hands on my mother, but I knew it was wrong just by hearing my mother cry and scream whenever they would fight. I feel like my father being in the streets was his therapy. Being in the streets to get away from his real-life problems. He used money to make the pain go away. It all just created more pain and confusion. Seeing my dad cry made me love him even more I have always loved my dad but expressing it only came easy by writing letters while he served time in jail and when my mother took my sister and I away from him.

My father was released from serving over nine years in prison in 2013. I thought he was done going to jail I even filled out countless job applications for him but addicted to fast money with no education and no real woman in his life he ended up right back in jail Super Bowl Sunday 2016. When he first went back to jail, I did not care because everything he promised during that federal bid, he got out and did the total opposite I felt like him going back to jail was his karma for letting me down and not keeping his word.

Honestly, my father has not had a fair chance at life, his mother was still a child when she gave birth to him. My father grew up around his uncles and money was easy to get they all sold drugs and raised hell in the city of Hallandale. Foster Road was their stomping grounds everybody knew the "Denmark's". My father has always moved to the beat of his own drum he is a leader of himself, it seems he can only be tamed by the system as opposed to just doing the right things to stay out of trouble. My father is not a bad father, but I would say he does not know how to be a father he does not even know how to talk to me because as I have gotten older and think about that phone conversation, his follow up question was pure ignorance when I told him about me being homosexual. My father is not a bad man, he just was never taught how to be a real man he is misunderstood probably to the point he may not even understand himself. Without a decent father figure in his life, he never had a clear shot at making something decent of himself. My father never grew up, his mentality is that of a little boy. God forbid if anything tragic was to ever happen to his mother, my dad will probably lose his complete mind. She is his rock the only one truly in his corner, the only one he can call on for anything no matter what he puts her through but again he is damn near 50 still leaning on his mother when it should be the other way around. At some point throughout his life, it should have clicked to my father to get his shit together if not for himself than for his children at least. It is crazy as much as I wanted to and attempted to have a strong relationship and a bond with my father, he always seemed to blow me off as if I am just not important to him. No advice, no life talks, nothing, he is just my "daddy" and that is all it seems he wanted me to know. My father only cares about money and females that mean him no good that is exactly how I see it because every female I have seen my father with is a low life just like him he does not have any standards and neither do the females he chooses to have dealings with. Any woman that does not encourage her man to do better and take care of his children is a deadbeat in my eyes. Every female I have seen my dad deal with including my mother, they were all users they used him for his money and did not encourage him to be a father to his children they did not encourage him to get a real job and every time he ends up in jail, they have a new penis sliding between their legs in no time.

In October 2001, my father's then girlfriend decided to step out on him with another man and the monster I had seen once beat my mother was risen again. My father's girlfriend thought it would be smart to take me and her other children up to Tampa, FL one October weekend we left on a Friday to see the guy she was cheating on my dad with. To make matters worse, when we got back on the road to head back the very next night to South Florida to answer an emergency call the guy came with us. Once we got back home in Dania Beach, FL late that Saturday night early Sunday morning we were unable to get inside the house. My father had locked the doors and the way that front door was setup certain locks could only be locked and unlocked from the inside like in a hotel room but not quite it was a bit more complicated SWAT team needed to break it down complicated. My father's girlfriend was too scared to enter the house in darkness through the back door she felt like my dad had setup a trap to kill her. She admitted to being fearful not wanting to enter the home without the assistance of the police. Instead of calling the police at that moment, we got back into the vehicle and headed to Hallandale. My father's girlfriend wanted clarity from her family as to why my dad had the heavy locks on the door, she was convinced that her mom ratted her out for free crack. Not too many people knew we went to Tampa, his girlfriend only told certain people like her drug addicted mom not thinking that she would tell my dad what was going on, but you can never trust a crack head especially if a free high is involved. We got to Hallandale and not even five minutes of being parked in front of Hallandale Cemetery talking her older sister, we seen my dad's white Buick reverse out of his girlfriend's mom parking lot. She panicked placed the car in drive attempting to escape his rage, she made a right turn onto

Pembroke Road and sure enough my dad was on his way right towards us. I remember being in the back of the rented Chevy Blazer SUV I was not sitting in an actual seat so no I was not wearing a seatbelt. The seats had been positioned down to give the children room and space to lay down in the back. As I looked out the back window facing west as the vehicle headed east, I seen my dad speeding up right behind us with a look in his eyes that I will never forget. I was banging on the window hoping that he could see me through the tints, I screamed repeatedly, "Daddy no! Daddy no! Daddy no!", I braced myself for the impact. After my father continuously rammed into the back of the vehicle numerous times his girlfriend kept driving, I honestly thought we were all going to die I thought the SUV was going to flip over especially after her glasses got knocked off her face from the impacts. I heard her yell repeatedly, "I can't see!", at that point the guy whom she was cheating with grabbed control of the stirring wheel while she kept her foot on the gas. My father chased us from Pembroke Road up until Federal Highway and Hallandale Beach Boulevard. After my father was no longer behind us, we ended up in a neighborhood near Aventura where some good Samaritans helped us out by calling the police. I was 11 years old and my life could have ended that night all because of my father's jealously not knowing how to control his emotions loving with his heart and not his mind. Later Sunday I spoke to my father and told him "you tried to kill us!", he told me he did not know anyone else was in the car he was only trying to kill his girlfriend. I am just thankful God had a shield of angels surrounding me that night, for that I know I am here today alive for a purpose I have a mission to accomplish. My dad is a liar deep down I know he knew myself and the rest of his children with that woman was in the vehicle when he attempted to run that SUV off the road, but he did not care he was ready and willing to take our lives and spend the rest of his life in jail all over a broken heart, I cannot respect it because no one on this Earth is worth that amount of energy.

So, I think to myself repeatedly had my father been blessed with a real father figure in his life chances are things may have been different for him. My father is one of the many little boys out here trapped inside a man's body. I pray that one day he gets it right before he ends up spending the rest of his life in jail all because he wants to chase behind fast money and tail that shit is really hell on a dead-end road to nowhere.

6
DIDN'T ASK TO BE HERE

My mother was sixteen and my father was seventeen when they conceived me, babies having a baby, they were not trying but they still made me. I came into this world automatically projected a failure by the system simply because of my DNA. As far back as I can remember I have never experienced my parents having an actual relationship, co-parent or other, and in a sense, it impacted me deeply leaving me scarred and heartbroken subconsciously. It made me a toxic individual I did not realize the damage until adulthood my late twenties. My mother was just a young girl roaming this free world looking for love and acceptance, so she got caught up with a street nigga. My father, the little boy trapped in a man's body, he did not know what he was doing my mother was just another body. When I was sixteen my mother told me, she wished she had aborted me and when I was twenty-four my father expressed that had he not been involved with my mother then I would have never been here. My response to both their remarks is this, but I did not ask to be here. I do not believe in coincidences, so I know I was placed on this Earth for a reason I deserve to be here, so I am going to make it all count. I am an unhuman being in human form.

According to Diana Baumrind, authoritarian parenting is restrictive, punitive style in which parents exhort the child to follow their directions and respect their work and effort. The authoritarian parent places firm limits and controls on the child and allows little verbal exchange. My mother's style of parenting for me could be described as authoritarian, so much so it forced me to run away from her home when I was only sixteen. As previously stated, my father was a street nigga, he has been either selling drugs or sitting in jail all of my life, and my mother realized early that was not the life she wanted for herself, so she moved away to a small city in Georgia outside of Valdosta and Macon. My mother was very strict on my sister and I growing up, it was worse than boot camp and I spent time in the military and my basic training does not come close to the experience I had under my mother's dictatorship. My mother is a member of the Nation of Islam and I can honestly say I felt like I was living in hell coming up in a Black Muslim household. I remember at eight years old my mother chastised me four times in one day all because I was crying, I wanted to move back to Florida to be with my father's family and in her words, she said, "I'm going to give ya ass something to cry for". In my mother's household we were under "rank and file" orders, we had to ask permission to do everything, "can I use the restroom?", "can I come out of the room?", those are just real-life examples of the things my sister and I was forced to do under the roof of my mother and her deranged husband. Every move made and every action taken had to be approved or else my sister and I would be chastised fully not with bare hands but with belts and switches (small tree branch). Today that would be considered as child abuse. Living life as a Muslim we did not eat pork but at the same time my mother did not provide us with lunch to take to school either.

One day my sister admitted to chowing down a sausage sandwich at school breakfast and my mother literally brushed my sister's teeth and gums with hand soap. By the time I was nine years old, I had become immune to the almost daily chastisements, so I started counting the hits and after about the sixth or seventh strike to my body I would begin to pretend like I was crying very dramatically and that would be her que to stop because she would hit us until we started crying, just feeding her ego. After my mother lightened up on physically beating us, she decided to make my sister and I do knee bends (squats), frog hops, and stand on one leg with both arms out (the star), as punishment. I am all for discipline, but had I been smarter as a child I would have reported my mother and her husband for child abuse. I was not a bad child at all I did what I was told and made decent grades in school, but it seems it just was not enough for my mother. As I have gotten older, I realize and understand that mental illnesses exist, so the actions and behaviors displayed by my mother were merely a reflection of her issues within herself. My mother went as far as taking my sister and I to a psychiatrist for evaluation as her reasoning for doing it was, she felt like my sister and I were mentally ill because we did not want to live with her. One of the last two beatings I received was at the age of fourteen from my mother and her husband. They both took turns beating up on me because I told her husband the magic words, "you're not my daddy!", my body was purple and blue after what felt like fifteen to twenty minutes of scuffling in real time. At sixteen years old, disgusted, and tired of my mother's antics I decided to speak up for myself and my sister by telling her, "you don't have to act like this towards us!", my mother charged at me beating me with her fists and pulled out a lot of my hair leaving patches. The police were called that night for the first time and she forced me to give her the retainers I was wearing for me to make the phone call for my granddad to come pick my sister and I up, my mother basically kicked us out of her house. To this day my mother says that I made the choice to leave her house and quite honestly if me giving her back my retainers was making a choice to leave her house then cool that is one of the best decisions I have ever made, I was finally free.

Baumrind states that neglectful parenting is a style in which the parent is uninvolved in the child's life. Although my father has spent a great deal of my life in and out of jail, I would describe his parenting style as neglectful. My father can be described as a "street nigga", all about his money and if it is not about the money, he has no real concern for it, well at least that is how he behaves. Ever since a child I always knew my father was a drug dealer, but he would always lie and say he cuts grass basically saying he was a landscaper without using the correct term. I consider my father to be neglectful because instead of spending quality time with my sister and I, he would leave us with one of his girlfriends or my grandmother to babysit while he ran the streets. I remember visiting him in prison once when I was sixteen and my father did not know how old I was, it hurt my feelings. The one and only time my father chastised me was because I made fun of him being dumped by his girlfriend when I was twelve years old. My father never showed interest in my academics nor did he encourage me to be my greatest self. My father told me that I did not need to go back and enroll in college because I was already living my life and school would just "slow you down". When my sister graduated from college, my father had the opportunity to spend time with all four of his biological children at once in about fourteen to fifteen years but instead, he flew him and his new girlfriend out to the graduation and treated it like a romantic getaway. He had just been released from serving ten years in prison. When I was seven years old, I observed my father go back and forth verbally on the phone with one of my aunts stating that "if ain't nobody there to pick them up they'll be left outside of the front door", we were in his care for the weekend and he was ready to finally get rid of us that Sunday afternoon. My father was very neglectful, he had a chance to receive sole custody of me when I was thirteen. The only thing he had to do was prove paternity to the Broward County court because my mother took a very nasty low blow in the custody hearing and told the judge "I don't know if he's the father", when it seemed as if the battle was not going in her favor. My father would not take the test to gain custody rights, so I was forced to move back to Georgia right after my thirteenth birthday.

As you can see, I was on a roller coaster ride with no seatbelts with both my parents and at this moment in my life I have no communication with either of them. One took being strict overboard and the other did not even bother trying to be a parent, they both should have never matted with each other, but I guess everything happens for a reason because I am here to help shape and mold the culture into to something even greater than it already is. I have always held a strong mind feeling as if I should not have been able to understand and see certain things so early in life. My innocence was tainted early, and it traumatized me all I wanted was for my parents to love my sister and I as oppose to being selfish pushing us off because they were not romantically involved. My mother and father behaviors towards us only showed me how not to be, due to my parents' actions it motivated me to be greater and it forced me to be independent.

At the age of twenty-eight, I do not have any children of my own, as I am a same gender lover. In my last relationship, my partner came with a package in the form of a little human and from day one I was in full parent mode. I raised that little girl from the time she was six months up until a few weeks before her fourth birthday. According to Baumrind, authoritative parenting encourages children to be independent but still places limits and controls on their actions. Extensive verbal give-and-take is allowed, and parents are warm and nurturant toward the child. My style of parenting could be described as authoritative, I was not too nice but at the same time I was not too mean either, I balanced it well. Strongly observing my parents' style of parenting, I just knew I wanted to be better than them and I have been, as a parent I was patient and a more effective communicator. As a parent I encouraged my daughter to talk to me and to tell me what was on her mind, I was there to guide her and to protect her, she knew I was not her biological parent, but I made her feel secure enough to call me "mommy" without ever placing that pressure on her. I was able to help my daughter become advanced enough to be accepted into pre-kindergarten sooner than her projected start date. The unconditional love I experienced being in that young child's life is what motivated me to be a better parental figure than my own parents, the love children give is real and all they truly need is love, patience, and to know that someone is in their corner. As an authoritative parental figure my daughter had a voice and was free to express herself as oppose to being placed in a box like I was while growing up. Being a parent there should be balance and I feel that taking on the role of being an authoritative parent is where you can find that balance. At the end of the day no one walking this Earth asked to be here so therefore children should be treated and cared for like the important humans that they are by their parents and all adults present in their lives.

7
BEGINNING STAGES OF LEARNING THYSELF

"Everyday Use by Alice Walker" is a story that I can probably relate to the most out of all the works I have read throughout the semester. Not by choice, I grew up in a Black Muslim household following the teachings of Elijah Muhammad, a teacher in the Nation of Islam. My mother moved to Georgia and married a Muslim man that influenced her to change her way of life. I was seven years old when I was introduced to Islam and I absolutely hated having to live under very strict rules and adapting to cultural changes I was not accustomed to like not eating certain foods and not celebrating holidays. It was not until I became an adult that I grasped my own understanding to the things I had been taught practically my whole life.

Being that the religion was forced on me I resented my mother for a very longtime and my stubbornness kept me from understanding and knowing valuable information at an early age. At the age of twenty, something happened to me, talks of the "illuminati" became more prevalent. Almost every conversation I was a part of someone always mentioned the New World Order, selling souls, blood sacrifices, demonic symbolisms, and masonry. I am more of an observer than a speaker so I would just listen but as time moved on certain things made me think and I decided to start researching on my own to gain my own knowledge and understanding. I connected the dots from the things that were taught to me as a child to things I learned on my own. Dee in "Everyday Use" is the character I would be because she gained knowledge of self, she became revolutionary, and she wanted better for her family.

Dee went off to college and gained knowledge of self which in turn made her appreciate being an African American woman. Whomever influenced Dee's new way of thinking taught her about her ancestors and the importance of the traditions brought over from Africa which is why she wanted the quilt and other things passed down from her grandmother and other family members, she was "black and proud" now. Unlike Dee, my mother is a conscious minded individual with a West Indian background, so she has always been proud to be Black which made me take a liking to certain African things like clothing and jewelry, and appreciating my ancestry was never an issue for me I always knew who I was in that sense and the importance of our uniqueness when it comes to style and different meanings. For example, the colors red, black, and green are colors with strong meanings behind them within the Black community. Red is for the blood our ancestors shed fighting for freedom, black is for our race, and green is for the stolen land. Dee has knowledge of self and so do I, I am proud of my nice brown skin tone and coursed hair because I know that I am of the original man which makes me a Goddess above all a spiritual being when you know the truth and when you know thyself that cannot be taken away from you. So, in all I can understand why Dee was so pressed about going home to collect those things she once despised and never cared for, like myself. I did not appreciate the knowledge placed on me as a child but now I am reading all books written by Elijah Muhammad and studying his lectures because his work is timeless, and he spoke on things that are going on right now in 2016.

I feel that Dee became revolutionary, not in a violent way but basically in a sense of knowing herself and wanted to spread that same knowledge for the betterment of her culture. Black empowerment does not mean White hate, so when Dee told her mom "your heritage" she basically meant it was time to let the slave mentality go and live as the queen she was placed on Earth to be. I am revolutionary as well my message is simple "handle yourselves accordingly and defend/protect yourself and those you love by any means", some consider it as being radical which I can understand but to those that know and understand we call it "being awake" or "having that third eye open". Black revolutionists are often misunderstood most times being called thugs, criminals, degenerates, crazy, and all things except the children of God when in my point of view, we just want equal justice under the law. So, when "black lives matter" is chanted it does not mean that no other life matters it simply means that black life matters too. Freedom, justice, and equality are all things that have been deprived from all people of color in America since Christopher Columbus "discovered" this land in 1492. The world would be a better place if all would realize that we are all one human race and it is easier to love than hate, God is above all. Dee did not mean any harm to her mom or Maggie she just was not able to get her point across without being insulting and it happens when you come into that new realm of revolutionism or better yet spirituality.

Dee wanted better for her family she said, "you just don't understand" I can relate because I feel the same way about my family, they called me crazy and still do at times for speaking about the things that I talk about not understanding that I am giving them valuable information because it is my duty to spread the message of survival and empowerment to those I love. As time has moved on, I am starting to realize that my family is somewhat taking heed to things that I say being that almost everyday something horrific is happening in the world. Nowadays I speak about global warming a lot and what is to come as sea levels continue to rise, me sharing that knowledge has influenced my aunt to buy property in the middle part of the United States being that Florida and coastal states will be no more if something is not done about the rapid melting of the ice in Antarctica. I have influenced my family to eat healthier and drink more water as those are the keys to a long life with regular exercise. I am the Dee in my household sharing knowledge is my way of showing love.

"Everyday Use" is a good story it shows how Dee evolved into loving herself and wanted to share her new way of life with her family. I am more like the character Dee because I have knowledge of self, I am revolutionary, I am spiritual, and I want better for my family with each day that passes. Dee was always an eccentric individual just like myself, so I can understand the dislike for her character because she was not meant to be liked by everyone. I have lost a lot of friends practically all my friends due to my evolvement and isolation from people and things I have outgrown, Dee's mom and sister Maggie are not ready to accept Dee for who she is just yet but as time moves on and Dee take a softer approach and stop being so self-centered it is possible that her family would understand. It was not easy for me at first talking to my family about my state of mind but now we all can agree to disagree on certain things and move on without hate or strife.

8

WE MATTER

As a millennial, when I chose to write about the Watts Riot the first thing that came to mind was the brutal beating of Rodney King, and how the acquittal of four officers, who were clearly seen on camera using unnecessary force, caused an uproar in the city of Los Angeles resulting in five days of rioting. After extensive research I have come to fully learn that there was an actual Watts Riot that took place in 1965 when a police officer conducted a traffic stop due to suspicion of an individual driving while intoxicated. Marquette Frye was his name, the African American motorist who was pulled over by Lee W. Minikus, a Caucasian California Highway Patrol officer on August 11, 1965 that led to six days of rioting in the Los Angeles, California neighborhood of Watts. We matter, we as in the oppressed people currently residing in North America, our ancestors were kidnapped, beaten, raped, and killed all in the name of making America great. The 1965 riot that took place in Watts, California was merely a demonstration showing just how tired and fed up the oppressed people were with the dominate society better known as our former slave master's children and grandchildren who continue daily to remind us that our lives are worthless due to the continuous harsh treatment the oppressed people are still faced with today. So, when you hear "Black Lives Matter", it does not mean that other lives do not matter it simply means that the oppressed people are just tired of being treated like they are less than human due their skin color.

Granted, according to Queally, Frye failed sobriety tests, so under the law he deserved to be arrested. The California Highway Patrol is to me what Florida State Troopers are to Floridians, officers patrolling the main highways not commonly seen in residential neighborhoods unless that is where they currently reside. As stated previously, Minikus was the Caucasian male who conducted the traffic stop, he supposedly responded to the report of a reckless driver, I'm confused as to why the LAPD did not conduct the stop since it happened in the actual neighborhood of Watts and not on the California highway I-5. It is no secret that before they were titled police officers the title was runaway slave patrol, so I understand the lack of enthusiasm when officers enter a predominately minoritized community, because most times the ending results are death and/or individuals being arrested. To eliminate racial tensions between police officers and the public I feel that police officers should police their own people. With a name like Minikus, I would not be surprised if he only stopped Frye, a twenty-one-year-old Black male, to intimidate a Black man because of his badge. In inner-city neighborhoods the only time you see a Caucasian is when they are in uniform and in the suburbs when you see a Black man he is labeled as a "thug" looking to rob somebody. Fyre was in the wrong for driving under the influence but Minikus is to be held liable too, as a highway patrol officer his business was not in the Watts neighborhood, in my opinion Minikus was looking for trouble. The statement made by a Cobb County cop, Greg Abbot, "But you're not Black. Remember, we only shoot Black people. Yeah, we only kill Black people, right?", is a good reason why I feel that each race of people should police communities where people that look like them frequent. Police officers are using minorities as target practice, requesting to only work in the ghetto because that is where all the fun is at.

According to Queally, a report issued by a state panel said that Frye had been talking and laughing with Minikus and other officers who had reported to the scene, but after his mother's arrival he began "cursing and shouting that they would have to kill him to take him to jail". From my personal experience dealing with law enforcement, it is very certain that Frye did not start acting out for no reason. I am sure with the presence of Frye's mother and stepbrother being on the scene, it made officers intimidated, feeling like they needed to exercise a more forceful authority over Frye in that moment which caused the madness to erupt. Yes, of course, before onlookers started arriving at the scene most likely Frye was cooperative and was obeying orders because they were given with respect. As stated from my personal experience with law enforcement personnel I know that officers tend to go overboard when there is an audience present. At the age of sixteen, I ran away from my mother's home and was placed under arrest. Initially the officer who arrested me was very respectful and spoke in a passive to assertive tone until I told him not to touch me in the way in which he proceeded. He grabbed and yanked my arm and slammed my 105-pound body against the wall placing me in handcuffs all because I asked him to not manhandle me. I was not even paying attention to the gathered crowd outside being nosey. I was charged with obstruction of justice for saying "you don't have to grab me like that", while trying to pull my arm back from the officer because that amount of force was unnecessary. I was cooperating fully, and I was not resisting arrest. I understand completely how Sandra Bland was feeling on

July 10, 2015 when she was pulled over and arrested for ultimately trying to exercise her natural human right to protect herself from unnecessary excessive force, better known as an unlawful arrest. Not only did Frye get arrested but his mother who came to retrieve his vehicle from being towed and his stepbrother were also arrested, according to the California Constitution and the First Amendment to the United States Constitution, we as citizens of the United Snakes of America, oops, I mean the United States of America, have the right to freedom of speech. I have not found any reports stating that Frye struck any officer but according to Queally, "after resisting arrest an officer swung his baton at Frye's shoulder and missed, landing on his head instead causing bleeding" and that strike caused the eruption of chaos that led to the six-day riot.

According to Civil Rights Digital Library, the Watts Riot of 1965 led to the deaths of thirty-four people, with more than a thousand reported injuries, and close to four thousand arrests. For real change to take place, there must be an uprising of the people. A revolution must take place and there will be casualties. When I think about the history of this country (The United States), July 4, 1776 is when America gained its independence from Great Britain. It was not given; it was earned through years of battle in the American Revolution. The Haitian Revolution to date is still known as the most successful slave rebellion in the Western Hemisphere, not only just ending slavery in Haiti but also according to blackpast.org, it also ended French control over the colony. To be liberated from oppression a fight must take place. Freedom has never been handed over without a price to pay and sometimes that price is death, jail, or injury. Freedom is not free, and the crowd in that Watts neighborhood on August 11, 1965 obviously understood that and was ready to risk it all. In my opinion those individuals made a choice to fight for their freedom, they fought to show unity and togetherness amongst each other. Give me liberty or give me death is the mentality that rioters exercised throughout those six days of rioting. Although I do not condone thievery and the ignorance that was displayed, I understand why those people did what they did. They were living in poverty with little to no employment on top of constantly being treated like less than human because of their skin tone. According to Los Angeles Times, for some people, like Gwendolyn Butler who lived near the focal point of the Watts Riot, it gave her a voice to speak up for herself. A Caucasian woman tried cutting in front of Butler in a bus line stating that the reason she was trying to skip the line was because "I'm White". After the Caucasian woman made that statement, Butler told her, "you're in the wrong place" and the White woman proceeded to the back of the bus line. The Watts Riot of 1965 may have given the darker race a voice to stand up for themselves, but that voice only made the dominant society of America fear the oppressed people more and forced them to not think twice about killing Blacks if need be using imminent danger as an excuse to commit murder amongst humans who clearly have the right to freedom of speech. It is crazy we live in a world where our words can get us killed. Look what happened to Malcolm X and Dr. Martin Luther King Jr., may both souls rest in peace.

All lives matter, Black lives matter, we matter, and if you ask me, I feel that if you are a part of the 99% population than at any given moment the 1% population can exterminate you if you are deemed to be a threat to the agenda, so in that case the 99% population matters. August 11, 1965 was the beginning of the end of the Civil Rights Movement because the oppressed people used their voices and different demonstrations to exercise change. They fought back, they showed fearlessness towards the dominant society. Fifty-three years later, we are still at the end of the Civil Rights Movement fighting for freedom, justice, and equality for all humans and not just Blacks. In the grand scheme of things, it is the Blacks that have suffered the most tyranny worldwide. In the words of Jesse Williams at the 2016 BET Awards, "just because we're magic doesn't mean we aren't real". When I first heard those words, my soul was touched, and it make me appreciate the sacrifices that have been made for people who look like me to be where we are today. We as Blacks may not have the full equality of those in the dominant society, but with the actions of those taken on August 11, 1965 through August 16, 1965 we are much further than we were and it's on my generation, the Millennial Nation, to help get us over that hump to true freedom, justice, and equality. After the Frye's were detained, police arrested a man and a woman in the crowd on allegations that they had incited violence. Whether those allegations are true or untrue, the fact of the matter is that those Watts residents were tired and fed up with inadequate schools, high unemployment rates, substandard housing, on top of constantly being harassed and treated worse than dogs by the dominant society so they fought. Give me liberty or give me death because we matter.

9
JESSE WILLIAMS INSPIRED ME TO BE GREATER

Jesse Williams is someone who I feel is noteworthy.

Mr. Williams is more than just "Dr. Jackson Avery" on *"Grey's Anatomy"*.

He is an advocate for the people a selfless servant of the world.

I can admit I did not know who Jesse Williams was until he received the 2016 Humanitarian Award at the BET Awards over the summer.

Jesse Williams is someone who has given me a sense of hope and inspiration to continue my journey letting me know that it is ok to feel how I feel and to believe what I believe because he feels the same way and share the same beliefs as me.

A biracial individual his mother is white, and his father is black, throughout his life Jesse Williams has been able to see and witness firsthand how both races talk about each other leaving him to become the man that he is today.

Using his platform, he has chosen to shed light on things others will not ordinarily speak about

Jesse Williams does not just speak for black people he speaks on things that every living human needs to hear and act on, especially in North America.

Mr. Williams has used social media to remind us that his celebrity status means nothing in a society where people are stigmatized and trivialized simply because of the color of their skin, sexuality, and/or religion.

Often compared to Harry Belafonte for his outspokenness about civil rights issues, Mr. Williams is one of today's notable civil rights activists.

He does not just speak about it he is about it.

Jesse Williams name is attached to different civil rights advocacy groups helping to shape the lives of the future leaders of tomorrow.

Jesse Williams is the youngest member of the board of directors at "The Advancement Project", a multiracial civil rights organization rooted in the great human rights struggles for equality and justice.

He is also the executive producer of "Question Bridge: Black Males", a multifaceted media project and website focused on the black male identity and the diversity within the demographic.

In the words of Jesse Williams "just because we're magic doesn't mean we aren't real".

Jesse Williams is a native of Chicago who graduated from Temple University earning a bachelor's degree in African American Studies and Film and Media Arts

After graduating college Jesse began teaching in low-income Philadelphia Public Charter Schools.

He was a high school teacher for six years teaching courses such as American History, African History, and English.

This is just a small synopsis to me on why Jesse Williams is noteworthy.

Mr. Williams is someone whom I inspire to be like in my own right as I have dreams to one day to become a teacher and an actress all while staying true to myself and never forgetting where and who I come from.

Jesse Williams's mother is Swedish, and his father is a Black Seminole, growing up he was taught the history that was not taught in school which is what inspired him to grow up advocating black lives and the problems with our justice system in America.

10

THE ELECTORAL COLLEGE

The 2016 election left a lot of people speechless and wondering what the heck is the Electoral College.

According to an article by NBC Los Angeles a majority of Americans from all backgrounds struggled to come up with the correct answers in a quiz about American history by the Intercollegiate Studies Institute. More than 2,500 randomly selected Americans took ISI's basic 33 question test on civic literacy and 71% of them received an average score of 49% or an "F." 43% did not know the Electoral College is a constitutionally mandated assembly that elects the president. One in five thinks it "trains those aspiring for higher office" or "was established to supervise the first televised presidential debates."

The Electoral College is the major key and only key in deciding who will be president of the United States.

Today I would like to define what the Electoral College is, how the Electoral College works, and why is the Electoral College important.

Government in America defines Electoral College as a unique American institution created by the Constitution, providing for the selection of the president by electors chosen by the state parties. Although the Electoral College vote usually reflects a popular majority, less populated states are overrepresented and the "winner-take-all" rule concentrates campaigns on close states.

The Huffington Post says that the Electoral College is made up of 538 electors who cast votes to decide the President and Vice-President of the United States. When voters go to the polls on Tuesday, they will be choosing which candidate receives their state's electors. The candidate who receives the most electoral votes (at least 270) wins the Presidency.

The National Conference of State Legislatures states that the Electoral College is a unique method for indirectly selecting the President of the United States.

The Electoral College consists of 538 electors, the elector is nominated by his or her state party committee or the elector campaigns for a spot and the decision is made during a vote held at the state's party convention.

Forty-eight out of the fifty states employ a winner-take-all system in which all their electors are awarded to the presidential candidate who wins the most votes statewide.

In Maine and Nebraska, they use the district system, an elector is allocated for every congressional district won, and whoever wins the state wins the two electors allotted to the state for its senators. For example, in 2008, Obama won the congressional district around Omaha, Nebraska, whereas McCain won the other two districts and the overall state vote. Therefore, Nebraska's electoral vote ended up being split with four electoral votes for McCain and one for Obama.

Electors meet in their states in December, following the November election, and then mail their votes to the vice president (who is also the president of the Senate). The vote is counted when the new congressional session opens in January and is reported by the vice president.

It introduces a bias into the campaign and electoral process. Because each state gets two electors for its senators regardless of population, the less populated states are overrepresented. The main reason Bush won the electoral vote in 2000 without winning the popular vote is because he did better in small states.

The final reason the Electoral College is important is because of the winner-take-all norm means candidates will necessarily focus on winning a relatively small number of battleground states, where the polls show that the contest is likely to be closest. The residents in battleground states are much more likely to see the ads and to have the candidates and their top ambassadors come to persuade them to get their vote.

So, it is not that your vote does not count, your vote just gives the electors an idea on who to give their electoral vote to and unfortunately although Broward County votes may have been majority Democratic the state of Florida voted Republican this past election.

As I close it is important that you all know that Trump did not cheat, he had a strategy to win and he won. The Electoral College is the deciding factor on who will be the president. I would suggest that if you do not like what is going on get involved not necessarily politically but become more active in your community and get to know the representatives representing you and your family in Washington, D.C. because moving out of the country will not solve your problems.

11

THE BELOVED WE CALL HER AMERICA

Question: "What role has isolationism historically played in American foreign policy, and what changes have taken place that makes isolationism less tenable today?"

Historically, the role isolationism has played in American foreign policy is that up until World War I, America stayed out of conflicts between other nations that they held no territory in, mainly Europe. America could maintain its isolationism by having power and/or control of territories in the Caribbean and in both Central and South America. The presence of the U.S. military plays a huge role in maintaining isolationism around the globe due to their intimidation tactics and being holders of the greatest amount of wealth around the world along with Europe and China. My personal belief is that since this country was founded by foreigners, automatically America must intervene in most of the world's affairs seeing as such there has been so many U.S. military interventions in both Central and South America and in the Caribbean since 1900. For me it all goes back to the start of the nation (United States), America has been fighting in wars since day one and as the world population continues to increase and the need for resources is in demand it makes it difficult for the 1%, or the few families that currently is in possession of the world's greatest wealth, or better yet the internal (elite) government within the government to control the world. To maintain power America and Europe had no choice but to establish the United Nations to maintain world peace and less chaos around the globe.

The change that has taken place in recent decades that makes isolationism less tenable today is the yarning of independence and freedom the Middle Eastern countries want from both the United States and Europe as a nation. The so-called terrorist attack on September 11, 2001 against the U.S. would be the latest threat towards isolationism to date, the country has been taking innocent lives since March 2003 in the Middle East and it has led to the expansion of Isis as they are on the quest to conquer the world and spread Islam. Isis has allegedly been behind many attacks such as the Paris attacks and the attack in Brussels at an airport, leaving other nations to come together and join forces with the U.S. to combat the terrorism of Isis. Although America as a country is the greatest place to be on Earth there will have to be a shift in power, real power to gain world peace. I must say the prophesies spoken upon in the Bible are playing out right in front of our eyes, this is truly the beginning of "the end". Isis is the new Soviet Union or communist group, and they will not go out without a fight which is why President Trump has been adamant about banning citizens from seven Muslim countries not including the ones he has personal business with. President Trump has joined forces with Russia to maintain the peace between them and the United States of America, and the Asian nation will continue to have America's favor particularly China as they now have in their possession nuclear weapons of their own that can potentially destroy America. America's independence is at risk and they are desperately trying to maintain its superiority by any means in every corner of the Earth amongst the oppressed including right here in the United States amongst the oppressed people on this soil whether it be the Indians, Hispanics, or African Americans there is a fight for justice and equality everywhere today.

12

BLACK ORATOR IMPACTING AFRICAN AMERICAN LIVES

"Turner was the last of his clan, mighty men mentally and physically, men who started at the bottom and hammered their way to the top by sheer brute strength, they were the spiritual progeny of African chieftains, and they built the African church in America"- W.E.B Du Bois; *The Crisis Magazine*

Being a part of a family that are members of the African Methodist Episcopal Church and my personal views on the liberation of blacks are reasons why I selected Henry McNeal Turner for research because he is someone, I knew nothing about until now. Turner was born into a free black family in February 1834 in South Carolina, as a child he worked beside slaves in cotton fields until he began working as a janitor. While working as a janitor at Abbeville Law Firm, due to his natural intelligence and ambition he was taught how to read and write. Shortly after learning how to read and write Turner received his license to preach and became a pastor in his late teens to early twenties for the Southern Methodist Church attracting large crowds filled with blacks and whites. Henry McNeal Turner's contribution in expanding the African Methodist Episcopal (AME) Church throughout the southern states of North America and being the first black Chaplin in the US armed forces is worthy of praise and recognition. Mr. Turner was also a man who preached truth and wanted to see an oppressed people set free. He was the heir to Fredrick Douglas and was the leading advocate for blacks to migrate back to Africa before the national uprising of Marcus Garvey.

In 1857, Turner left the Southern Methodist Church and joined a church controlled exclusively by black men. The African Methodist Episcopal Church (AME) is the church he first learned of while doing evangelist missionary work in New Orleans, LA. After extensive training, Mr. Turner was assigned to preach at Israel Church on Capitol Hill located in Washington, DC; the largest AME Church in the city. Not only did he attract black audiences with his flamboyant preaching but government officials as well. After the Emancipation Proclamation was issued in 1863, Mr. Turner helped recruit black men to enlist in the First United States Colored Troop (USCT) regiment to fight in the Civil War. In return for his help in recruiting the black troops, Turner was appointed to be the first black chaplain in the US Armed Forces by President Abraham Lincoln.

During the Civil War, Turner's love for journalism grew as he realized it was a powerful tool for reaching black people. As a writer for the *Christian Recorder* and occasionally the *Weekly Anglo-African* newspapers, Mr. Turner wrote about a variety of subjects. Subjects included race issues, church affairs, his personal concerns, and battle accounts. His detailed battle accounts attracted many readers for the style as well as the content because he accompanied his soldiers on the battlefield during missions. He wrote about the war from the perspective of black soldiers, describing their battles, praising their courage, and arguing with rivals and politicians.

The Little Infant Destined for Greatness

Two years of serving in the Armed Forces from 1863-1865 Mr. Turner found his life's work, realizing that writing for the public had its rewards. He garnered national attention throughout the AME church and black communities. After the Civil War he was assigned to the Freedman's Bureau in Georgia to help blacks' transition from slavery to freedom. Turner entered politics to act as a voice for blacks and to increase the AME membership within the black community after he resigned from the Freedman's Bureau because he found racial discrimination to be as strong as ever in Georgia. He worked with white Republicans to develop a multiracial coalition which would govern the South. Turner helped recruit black voters for the Republican Party and helped draft the new state constitution in 1867. He became a legislator in 1868 but was expelled with fourteen other black representatives in 1870 when they were out voted by the house and refused their seats. The rejection made him turn his back on politics. After his stint as a legislator, Turner served as postmaster in Macon, GA and a customs inspector in Savannah, GA. He had preferred working within all-black organizations rather than to endure the insults blacks were faced with in integrated settings.

Mr. Turner was the first Bishop of the AME Church in the South serving from 1880 until 1892. His true work was building the AME Church in the South, his aggression in speaking out against injustices earned much hate from whites but due to his fearless speaking the AME membership flourished. He was the first Bishop to ordain a woman by the name of Sarah Ann Hughes as Deacon in 1855 due to his belief on equal rights but reversed the decision due to sexist backlash within the AME Church. He worked strenuously building the AME membership and concentrated his efforts entirely on the church and black organizations. Even though black troops aided in the Civil War, there were no civil rights given to blacks during the reconstruction era and as it came to an end, to solve the racial injustice issues he had been faced with, Turner advocated the return of blacks to Africa "to achieve our dignity and manhood" he preached in one sermon. In 1898, he preached that "God is a negro" and African Americans should see him as such just like any other race seen God as their own and of course that did not sit well with whites especially the government. Mr. Turner received little to no support on his idea of emigrating back to Africa from fellow Bishops.

Turner visited Africa four times between 1891-1898. He organized four AME conferences in Africa to introduce more African Americans to the continent and organized missions in the colonies. He never planned to move to Africa permanently, unless thousands of other blacks migrated as well. The interest of moving to Africa was great but money was not available for the mobilization and building of a black nation.

Henry McNeal Turner transitioned into death on May 8, 1915. Although his radical alternative solution to the loss of black civil rights was not met with wide acceptance, a great migration did take place. During the 1910s and 1920s thousands of blacks migrated to the North from the South for better life opportunities. Mr. Turner helped set the tone for black advocates to use their voice and to speak on what needed to be said to motivate blacks to do better and want better for themselves. For as long as African Americans have been on this land, the United States has failed to uphold and defend the civil rights of black people. Henry McNeal Turner along with a host of other black activists only wanted and wants to see the black man and black woman set free from their oppressor. Justice is due, separation is the solution. Migrating back to Africa would not necessarily be necessary today for the culture but being able to police our own communities and generating wealth amongst each other without the interference of white supremacy and the race soldiers disguised as police would not be so bad if everyone were able to handle their own affairs basically a nation within a nation. As an African American being exposed to many different things primarily growing up as a Black Muslim in the Nation of Islam and the other half of my family being a part of the AME church, I feel as though Mr. Turner's views and intent greatly impacted the lives of conscious minded African Americans and motivated us as a race to do for self and to separate from a system that offers no justice to the oppressed. Mr. Turner was a pioneer that helped set the tone by preaching about the liberation of blacks and working within black organizations to find solutions to make us a better people. What is interesting to me about Mr. Turner personally is that he makes me want to do some digging into my ancestral background because his mother's maiden name I found out to be Green. It may be a possibility we are related someway because that is the last name of my biological father's family which to me explains the connection to the AME church and my grandfather having the first name of Richard most likely named after Richard Allen the founder of the AME church in 1816.

13

MOMMY TOO

In the year 2000 Census there were approximately 594,000 same-sex partner households. There were children living in approximately 27% of those households.

Do you all feel that children are better off with a father in prison than being raised in a home with lesbian parents and no father at all? Well in some ways same-sex parents may bring talents to the table that straight parents do not.

I researched more than what you would just find on gay bashing websites and in the numerous versions of the Bible rewritten by different scholarly individuals such as Shakespeare, supposedly stating that an alternative lifestyle is an abomination by God. No sin is greater than the other, I like to think of myself as a gatekeeper because I am love, I spread love, and I live my life in love. This is not about God because when you know thyself you know God and you know that God is love and when you live your life with a pure and genuine heart you have nothing to worry about because there is heaven and hell on Earth. It is all about how you treat others whether verbally or nonverbally control your thoughts and actions.

I am not here to tell you to join the club, but I do want you to feel okay and not pass judgement or stare uncontrollably the next time you see somebody that look or dress like me walking around the mall pushing a stroller or sitting in Benihana having lunch with my family because we are normal people just like you.

Same-sex parents are as good as straight ones, there are very little to no differences between children of same-sex and opposite-sex parents and I am going tell you how, and finally I am going to tell you what parenting life has been like for me.

To begin, being that the odds are automatically against anyone in a same-sex parenting relationship we go above and beyond to be the best parents we can be.

Abbie Goldberg, a psychologist at Clark University in Massachusetts who researches gay and lesbian parenting said that gay parents tend to be more motivated and more committed than heterosexual parents on average, because they chose to be parents. Gay couples cannot have an unplanned pregnancy, which causes them to scramble for resources and make sacrifices. Therefore, their children may live better lives.

Gay parents might be better at raising children because they are more often prepared, and they do not adhere to traditional gender roles. Household responsibilities are more than likely evenly distributed which leaves the same-sex family to get along better and in turn it has positive impacts on the child's mental health and overall behavior.

There are no major differences in children who are raised by same-sex parents and opposite-sex parents.

Research has shown that the children of same-sex couples both adopted and biological children fare no worse than the children of straight couples on mental health, social functioning, school performance and a variety of other life-success measures.

In a 2010 review of virtually every study on gay parenting, New York University sociologist Judith Stacey found no differences between children raised in homes with two heterosexual parents and children raised with lesbian parents. Stacey said that "there's no doubt whatsoever from the research that children with two lesbian parents are growing up to be just as well-adjusted and successful as children with a male and a female parent."

The only consistent place you find differences between how children of same-sex parents and children of opposite-sex parents turn out are in the issues of tolerance and open-mindedness. According to in-depth interviews conducted by Abbie Goldberg, forty-six adults with at least one homosexual parent felt like their perspectives on family, gender, and sexuality have largely been enhanced by growing up with gay parents.

Which leads me to my last and final point on what family life has been like for me for the past three years.

In 2014 at 24 years old I met someone who was engaged and had given birth just six months prior to a beautiful baby girl. Of course, we started off as friends not knowing where things would lead to. The moment I realized that things were a little more serious than I thought I had to accept everything that came with her including her child. From day one I have been dedicated and committed to my family, our number one priority is to provide her with everything that she needs while teaching her right from wrong and most importantly loving her unconditionally because she will not be punished for our decisions, we will give her the best life as possible and set her up for success as she continues to grow.

"Lil Kookie" is three years old full of life, very happy, and joyful with three individuals (her mother, father, and me) active and present in her life giving her the world because to us this is her world, and we are just living in it. At eighteen months we had her potty-trained to make up for all the time she spent for not wanting to walk until a few days before her first birthday. She is bilingual and knows pretty much all the basics a child should know that is in pre-k or kindergarten because we refuse to be statistics in a system that automatically places us as failures before we even try to accomplish great things.

Being a parent has been the most rewarding and precious gift I have ever received. My child has given me a new outlook on life and because of her I am more patient, and I am calmer, and everything I do is for her. Collectively between the three of us (mother, father, myself) we want her to have a life that we never had. Being that I am very doubtful that I will ever have a child of my own, the bond that we share and the love between us is unmatched and I would not trade it for nothing in this world, gaining a family saved me from going down the wrong path if it were not for my partner and our daughter honestly, I would probably be dead or in jail I made needed changes in my life because of them.

In conclusion, I feel that you all should be more open minded and not as judgmental when you see a same-sex family because you never know what the situation may be because more likely than none except for a deceased parent or incarcerated parent children from previous heterosexual relationships tend to have both parents in their life despite one parent being involved with or in a relationship with someone of the same-sex. Homosexual parents are just as good as straight ones. A lot of naysayers say that having same-sex parents have a negative impact on childhood outcome, but they are wrong.

The Little Infant Destined for Greatness

I told you all what parenting life has been like for me. At the end of the day, it is all about the child nothing is above raising the child in the safest and most nontoxic way as possible while making sure educationally and socially she/he meets and exceeds standards.

No one on this Earth asked to be here and there is no rule book on how to raise children all you really need is common sense and a sane mind, so whether you are for love or against homosexuality understand that when you see someone who appears to be gay or lesbian out in public be mindful of how you look at them or the thoughts that cross your mind because there is no rule or instruction stating that children can only be raised by one man and one woman remember it takes a "village" to raise a child.

In the year 2010 Census it is suggested that there are nearly 650,000 same-sex couples living in the United States and it is estimated that 19% of those households include children under the age of 18. That means that approximately 125,000 same-sex couples are raising nearly 220,000 children. Approximately 3 out of every 1000 children in the United States are living with a same-sex couple. Now that you have heard the numbers, the research, and actual testimony, I would hope that you do not frown upon a family that looks like mine the next time you see one in public.

ACKNOWLEDGMENTS

First and foremost, I want to thank God the creator of the universe for life and the continued protection over my life as I walk amongst this world. My mother, whom in which I was angry at and resented for a long time, I appreciate how far we have come since our last fallout in March of 2018. I love you and I am happy we have grown from that. I know if you read this book you may become saddened, you may have a different version of some of the events that have happened, and you may not remember some of things that took place. Always remember there is three-sides to every story, my side, your side, and the truth. I love you no matter what Mommy and by no means have I decided to put this information out to hurt you or to taint your image. I pray that our mother/daughter bond continues to grow and remain organic, your tough love paid off and I am indebted to you for a lifetime for all the lessons. To my partner Cristina, you gave me a new perspective on life in so many ways. Thank you for allowing me to be a part of the most important part of your life in raising your daughter, I love you both beyond what words could explain. You both saved me. Cristina you are my rock and I appreciate you for supporting me always in all ways that you possibly can. Thank you for believing in me and pushing me to go harder, you are my motivation. To my Auntie Tavie, you opened your doors and gave me a roof over my head with no stipulations on my sexual orientation. You freed me and allowed me to grow into my own. I appreciate you and I love you beyond life, thank you for everything you are my real-life fairy godmother. Auntie thank you for consoling me and reassuring me that the pain do not last long at all, despite all of the tears I have cried you always told me "I promise you it is going to be okay, you are going to be fine". From the messy breakups I have had to taking time out of your life to keep me from being arrested, thank you for always having my back I love you for all of that. Your accomplishments and perseverance through a tough life is my biggest inspiration. Auntie you deserve the world, and I will continue to cherish you for all the good you have done for me. To my daddy, I love you I love you I love you. I pray that you find real peace and happiness within yourself. I pray that as you grow older in age that you become wiser. Daddy I pray that you open up and be that spiritually awakened individual that you are on the inside, you are a King it is okay to showcase your mental growth it is okay to put the ignorance and the past behind you and become a new man. I wish things could have been different. To everyone else, close family and ones whom I call my friends my spiritual sisters and brothers I love you always. Thank you for the encouraging words, thank you for the positivity you bring into my life whether it is sharing a post to make me laugh or think or just information to feed my mind. Thank you for just wanting to overall see me do well in life. If you took the time out to read and/or purchase my book **THANK YOU** a million times over God Bless You and I wish you much peace, love, and prosperity.

CONTACT THE AUTHOR

Kashus "Kash" Peterson

IG: kashus__

Email: kashus.sereta@icloud.com

Website: www.kclgoodsllc.com

BIBLIOGRAPHY

Santrock, John W. (2018). Essentials of Life-Span Development, 5th edition. McGraw-Hill: New York, NY.

(2018). What is My Parenting Style? Four Types of Parenting. Retrieved from http://www.brighthorizons.com/family-resources/e-family-news/parenting-style-four-types-of-parenting.

Bates, Karen Grigsby. "When LA Erupted in Anger: A Look Back At The Rodney King Riot." National Public Radio, Inc, 2017, https://www.npr.org/2017/04/26/524744989/when-la-erupted-in-anger-a-look-back-at-the-rodney-king-riots.

Edy, Jill A. "Watts Riots of 1965 American History". Encyclopedia Britannica, Inc. 2018, https://www.britannica.com/event/Watts-Riots-of-1965.

"Haitian Revolution (1791-1804)." BlackPast.Org, 2007-2017, www.blackpast.org/gah/haitian-revolution-1791-1804.

Jennings, Angel and Mozingo, Joe. "50 years after Watts: 'There

Bibliography

is still a crisis in the black community'". Los Angeles Times, 2015, www.latimes.com/local/wattsriots/la-me-watts-african-americans-20150813-story.html.

Lopez, German. "" We only shoot black people," Georgia cop assures woman during traffic stop". 2017, https://www.google.com/amp/s/www.vox.com/platform/amp/identities/2017/8/31/16232880/georgia-police-cobb-county-video

Queally, James. "Watts Riots: Traffic stop was the spark that ignited days of destruction in L.A.". 2015, www.latimes.com/local.lanow/la-me-In-watts-riots-explainer-20150715-htmlstory.html

Rothman, Lily. "50 Years After Watts: The Causes of a Riot". TIME, 2015, https://time.com/3974595/watts-riot-1965-history/

"Watts Riot". Civil Rights Digital Library, 2018, http://crdl.usg.edu/events/watts_riots/?%20Welcome&Welcome&Welcome&Welcome.&Welcome

Clarendon, Dan. "25 Things You Didn't Know About Jesse Williams." Wetpaint, http://www.wetpaint.com/25-things-you-didnt-know-about-jesse-williams-641796/*

Fisher, Luchina. "5 Things to Know About Jesse Williams." ABC News, http://abcnews.go.com/Entertainment/things-jesse-williams/story?id=40167629*

"Jesse Williams." Advancement Project, http://www.advancementproject.org/people/entry/jessewilliams*

Bibliography

"Jesse Williams Bio." Answer, http://ans-wer.com/biography/jesse-williams-biography.html*

"Jesse Williams TV Actor" Famous Birthdays, http://www.famousbirthdays.com/people/jesse-williams.html*

Lasher, Megan." Read the Full Transcript of Jesse Williams' Powerful Speech on Race at the BET Awards." TIME, http://time.com/4383516/jesse-williams-bet-speech-transcript/*

Bonsor, Kevin and Dove, Laurie L. "How the Electoral College Works." How Stuff Works Culture, http://people.howstuffworks.com/electoral-college2.htm.

Edwards, George C., and Martin P. Wattenberg. "Government in America: people, politics, and policy". The Last Battle: The Electoral College PP. 303-304. Boston: Pearson, 2015. Print.

"Electoral College." History, http://www.history.com/topics/electoral-college.

Politics. "What is The Electoral College? How It Works and Why It Matters." The Huffington Post. 6 November 2012, http://www.huffingtonpost.com/2012/11/06/what-is-the-electoral college_n_2078970.html.

Prokop, Andrew. "Why the Electoral College is the Absolute Worst, Explained." Vox, 19 December 2016, http://www.vox.com/policy-andpolitics/2016/11/7/12315574/electoral-college-explained-presidential-elections2016.

"Study Americans Don't Know Much About History." NBC. 17 July 2009, http://www.nbclosangeles.com/news/local/Study-Americans-Dont-Know-About-Much-About-History.html.

Bibliography

"The Electoral College." NCSL, 22 August 2016, http://www.ncsl.org/research/elections-and-campaigns/the-electoral-college.aspx

Boyd, Herb. Autobiography of a People. (Henry McNeal Turner p. 164-167), 2000.

Simmons, Martha and Thomas, Frank A. Preaching With Sacred Fire. (Henry McNeal Turner p. 344-348), 2010.

Smith, John David. Black Soldiers in Blue African American Troops in the Civil War Era. (Henry McNeal Turner Black Chaplin in the Union Army by Edwin S. Redkey p. 336-360), 2002.

Sernett,Milton C.Afro-American Religious History. (Henry McNeal Turner Emigration to Africa p.260-266), 1985.

Felder, Cain Hope. "People of Faith: Henry McNeal Turner"PBS, www.pbs.org/thisfarbyfaith/people/henry_mcneal_turner.html.*

Martin, Jonathan. "Turner, Henry McNeal 1834–1915." Contemporary Black Biography http://www.encyclopedia.com.*

Angell, Stephen W. "Henry McNeal Turner (1834-1915)." New Georgia Encyclopedia. http://www.georgiaencyclopedia.org/articles/history-archaeology/henry-mcneal-turner-1834-1915*

Barlow, Rich. "Gay Parents As Good As Straight Ones." *BU Today,* 11 April 2013, https://www.bu.edu/today/2013/gay-parents-as-good-as-straight-ones/.

Bibliography

Gate, Gary J. "LGBT Parenting in the United States." *The Williams Institute, UCLA School of Law,* February 2013, www.law.ucla.edu/williamsinstitute.

Kounang, Nadia. "'No Differences' Between Children of Same-Sex and Opposite-Sex Parents." *CNN,* 15 April 2016, http://www.cnn.com/2016/04/15/health/health-of-children-with-same-sex-parents/.

Pappas, Stephanie. "Why Gay Parents May Be the Best Parents." *Live Science,* 15 January 2012, http://www.livescience.com/17913-advantages-gay-parents.html.

"Same-Sex Parents and Their Children." *AAMFT,* https://www.aamft.org/imis15/aamft/Content/Consumer_Updates_Samesex_Parents_and_Their_Children.aspx.

"What Does The Scholarly Research Say About The Wellbeing Of Children With Gay Or Lesbian Parents?" *Columbia Law School,* http://whatweknow.law.columbia.edu/topics/lgbt-equality/what-does-the-scholarly-research-say-about-the-wellbeing-of-children-with-gay-or-lesbian-parents/.

www.ingramcontent.com/pod-product-compliance
Lightning Source LLC
Chambersburg PA
CBHW071625170426
43195CB00038B/2126